A TEXTBOOK OF

ARTIFICIAL INTELLIGENCE

(Unlocking the Secrets of AI)

Subject Code: 901A| Skill Education

(As per Latest NEP Guidelines)

6
CBSE

Name ....

Class .... Section .... Roll No. ....

School ....

Address ....

Phone ....

Preeti Saxena

A TEXTBOOK OF

ARTIFICIAL INTELLIGENCE

(Unlocking the Secrets of AI)

Subject Code: 901A| Skill Education

(As per Latest NEP Guidelines)

Class VI

By:

Preeti Saxena

Suvigya Saxena

S.K. KATARIA & SONS®

Educational Publishers

4885/109, Prakash Mahal, Dr. Subhash Bhargav Lane,
Opposite Delhi Medical Association, Daryaganj, New Delhi-110002 (INDIA)
Phone: +91-11-43551243; Mobile: +91-9871775858, 7678425209
e-mail: katariabook@gmail.com; katariabooks@yahoo.com
Website: www.skkatariaandsons.com

(e-books, subscriptions and bulk buying also available on our website)

Published by:

S.K. Kataria & Sons®

4885/109, Prakash Mahal, Dr. Subhash Bhargav Lane,
Opposite Delhi Medical Association, Daryaganj, New Delhi-110002 (INDIA)
Phone: +91-11-43551243; Mobile: +91-9871775858, 7678425209
e-mail: katariabook@gmail.com; katariabooks@yahoo.com
Website: www.skkatariaandsons.com

First Edition: 2025; Second Edition: 2025-2026; Third Edition: 2026-2027

ISBN: 978-81-963589-3-8

Laser Typesetting by : S.K. Computers, Delhi

Printed at: Yash Printographics, Noida

PREFACE

Artificial intelligence (AI) has emerged as a new Technology Trend. It has reshaped industries and daily life. From self-driving cars to medical diagnoses, AI's applications are boundless. This book is an effort to bring the latest technology for students as a part of vocational education mentioned in NEP(New education Policy-2020). This book has all the latest features of AI with very interesting games that helps students to understand the technology in a better way. As AI continues to advance, it promises to further enhance productivity, personalize experiences, and drive innovation, bringing a transformative change in the technology of our time.

Class 6 (Skill module 901A) module has all the basic contents related to Artificial Intelligence like the difference between automation and AI, applications of AI, domains of AI with details of computer vision. Students will learn the process behind the working of an Artificial Intelligence device. They will be able to correlate human intelligence with artificial intelligence and how AI has made human difficult task simpler in real life. The book has Fun.AI activity for the students to learn and explore new AI world and some interesting Scooby-Doo quest for examining your skill.

This book has interesting videos, theoretical and objective type questions which are important for the assessment. These questions are given in the form of activity and games so that students can learn more. This book is an effort to teach and make you understand difficult topics in easy manner and simple language. Though it has been kept in mind that errors are not there but being human, even I can commit some errors. This is my request that if you come across any such problem, kindly inform me through my email katariabook@gmail.com.

Note: *CBSE Vocational Education Skill based (According to NEP-2020).*

Sources: *Internet and several online AI tools with games has helped us in framing our content. My thanks and gratitude to such sources.*

Preeti Saxena

ACKNOWLEDGEMENTS

My first and foremost thanks to my Almighty **'Sai Ram'**. During this journey from becoming a student to a teacher and now an author, my **'Sai Ram '** was with me throughout, inspiring me always to move ahead in life.He taught me that faith and hard work can give you everything you dream of.

I amalso grateful to my parents who made me a self independent person. They gave me higher education and moral values. My dad **Mr. Som Nath Gupta** and my mom **Mrs. Lajja Gupta**, taught me how to face challenges of life.

My sincere thanks to my students who believed in me and motivated me to write this book. They trusted me and guided me by giving words to my Knowledge. So I have tried my level best to share my knowledge on this subject with my students.

A special and heart filled thanks to my husband, **Mr. Sharad Saxena** and my son, **Suvigya** who compromised a lot during my journey as an author. They motivated me, trusted me and helped me in day-to-day working. I could have never, thought of writing this book without their support.

Last but not the least, I am grateful to my in-laws and friends who were constantly guiding me and giving me emotional and moral support during my work. I would also like to give my special thanks to one of my friend, **Mr. Ashish Bhargava**, who constantly motivated me to complete my work on time.

Preeti Saxena

PUBLISHER'S PREFACE

It is with immense pride and gratitude that we present this edition under the name of M/s S.K Kataria & Sons. We have recently been awarded with the **Best Publisher Award 2025 by DSBPA, Delhi.** Receiving this award reinforces our dedication to setting high standards in editorial quality, design and reader engagement.

This recognition stands as a testament to our unwavering commitment to quality, creativity and the pursuit of excellence in the world of publishing.

For us, publishing is more than producing books. It is more about nurturing ideas, empowering voices and building a bridge between esteemed authors and young readers.

Each book of our publication is a masterpiece and is driven by our passion for knowledge, innovation and literary integrity.

We extend our heartfelt gratitude to our esteemed authors, editors, designers and most importantly readers whose trust and enthusiasm continues to inspire us.

As you turn the pages of this book, we request you to share your valuable feedback with us.

Please Email us at **katariabook@gmail.com.**

With warm regards

Sanjeev Kataria

KATSON BOOKS

M/s. S.K. Kataria & Sons

New Delhi

Website: www.skkatariaandsons.com

Email: katariabook@gmail.com

WORK DETAIL

S.No.	Chapter Name	Date	Teacher's Signature

MY PERFORMANCE

Date	Text/ Exam	Marks/Grades Obtained			Highest Marks/Grade in the class	Teacher's Remarks	Parents Signature
		Theory	Practical	Total			

WORK DETAIL

S.No.	Chapter Name	Date	Teacher's Signature

MY PERFORMANCE

Date	Text/ Exam	Marks/Grades Obtained			Highest Marks/Grade in the class	Teacher's Remarks	Parents Signature
		Theory	Practical	Total			

CONTENTS

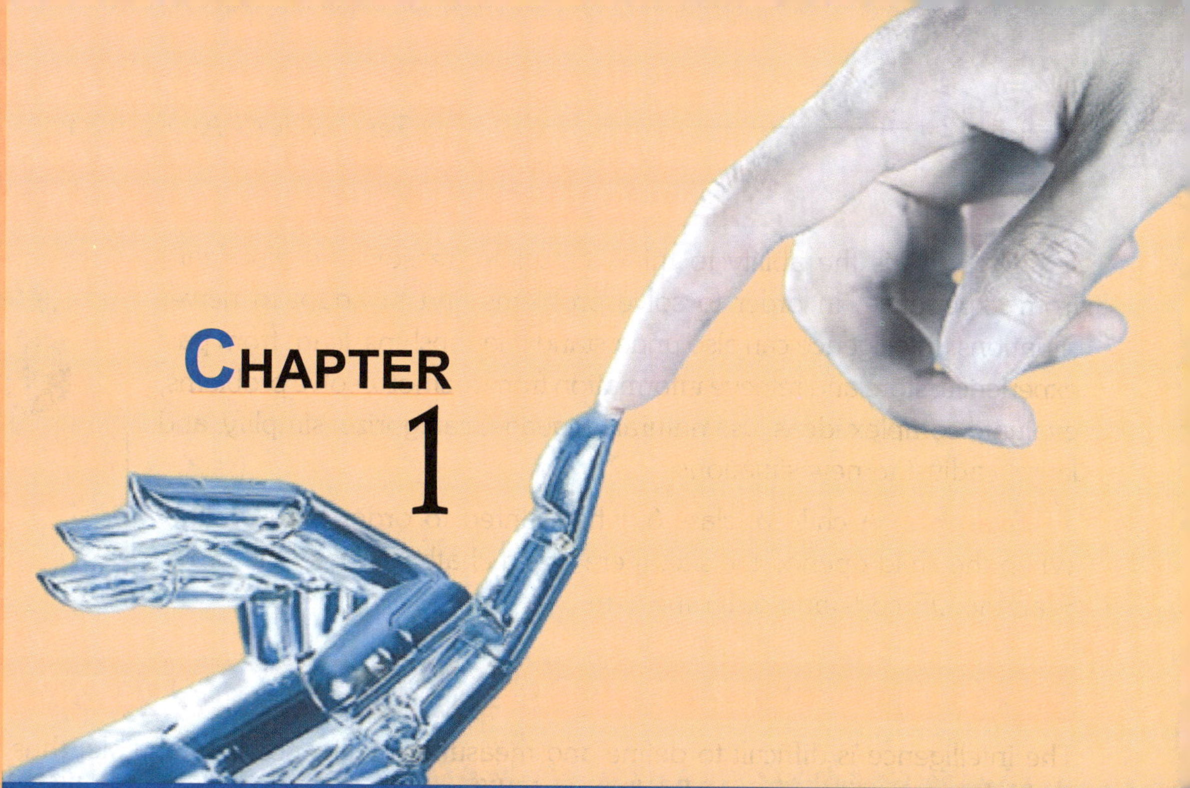

CHAPTER 1

GETTING STARTED WITH AI

Getting Started with AI
in Action

Scan QR Code

OBJECTIVES

TOPICS TO BE COVERED

- Introduction about Intelligence
- What is Intelligence made of?
- Types of Intelligence
- Difference between Human and the Machine Intelligence
- What is Artificial Intelligence?
- Understanding Artificial Intelligence
- Why we need Artificial Intelligence?
- How is Artificial Intelligence difference from automation?
- Advantages of Artificial Intelligence
- Disadvantages of Artificial Intelligence
- How Does AI Work?

1.1 INTRODUCTION ABOUT INTELLIGENCE

Intelligence is the ability to think, calculate, reason and also learn from experience, in order to solve problems and to adapt to newer situations. Intelligence can also understand relationships, learn from past experience, store and retrieve information from memory, solve problems, evaluate complex ideas, use natural language, categorize, simplify, and largely adjust to new situations.

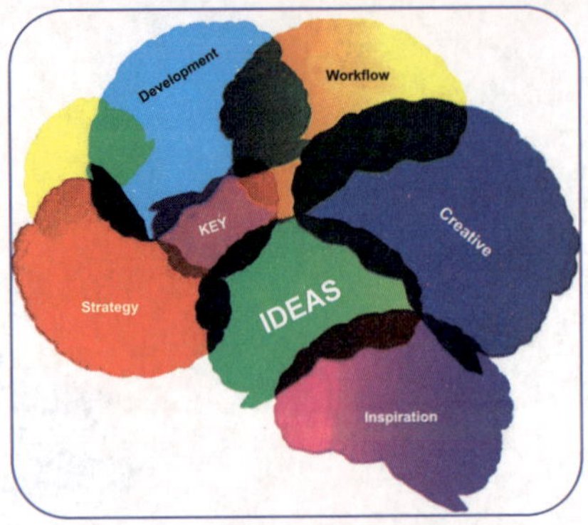

Example: A child of class 6, who wanted to order food, online. When the child opened the site, there was a chatbot to take the order. Scan the QR code and order the item.

1.2 WHAT IS INTELLIGENCE MADE OF?

The intelligence is difficult to define and measure. Intelligence is intangible, thus it varies from person to person . Intelligence is different for different person and different situations . Intelligence cannot be directly observed, touched, or measured in physical terms. However, we can still say that it is composed of:

- Reasoning,
- Learning,
- Problem Solving,
- Perception,
- Linguistic Intelligence.

Treasure Link
What is Intelligence? in Action
Scan QR Code

FUN.AI ACTIVITY

https://hellotars.com/chatbot-templates/restaurant-hotel/ry3eAc/zzungry-food-ordering-chatbot

Treasure Link
Ordering Food in Action
Scan QR Code

Scan and order the food you need using chatbot.

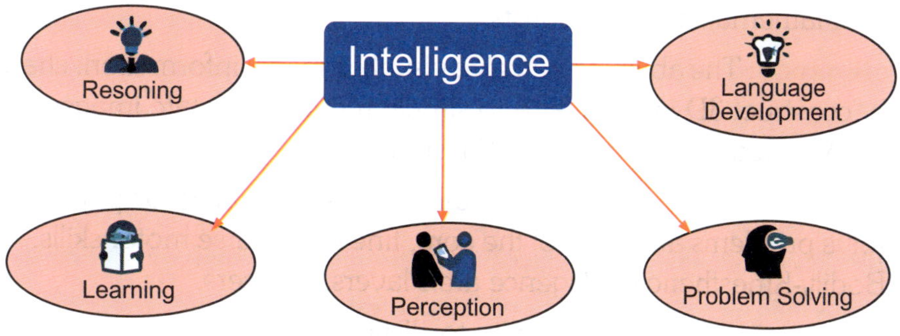

Let us go through all the components briefly:

- **Reasoning:** It is the complete set of processes that help us in providing a base for judging , making decisions, and predicting behaviour.
- **Learning:** It is the act of gaining full knowledge or skill by either studying the mechanism or by practicing a skill or being taught a concept or experiencing something around. Learning increases the awareness of the subjects of the study.

  The ability of learning is possessed by humans, some animals, and AI-enabled systems. Learning is of various types like **Auditory Learning** (through listening and hearing), **Episodic Learning** (through some sequences of events), **Motor Learning** (through movement of muscles), **Observational Learning** (through vividly watching others), **Perceptual Learning** (through sensory experience), **Relational Learning** (through relationship or relational properties), **Spatial Learning** (through visual stimuli) and also the **Stimulus-Response Learning** (through a particular behaviour).
- **Problem Solving:** It is the process in which one perceives and tries to then find a solution a current situation by following some path. Problem solving also involves **decision making**, where in one finds the best solution towards a given problem among the various alternatives available.
- **Perception:** It is the process of acquiring, analysing , interpreting, selecting, and also organizing sensory information. Perception presumes **sensing**. In humans, perception is derived from sensory organs. In terms of artificial intelligent , any perception mechanism puts the data derived from sensory organs in an organized manner.
- **Linguistic Intelligence:** It is one's ability to use, understand, evaluate, speak, and then write the verbal and written language. It is an important part of communication.

1.3 TYPES OF INTELLIGENCE

Intelligence can be of many types depending upon the skill a person has. Howard Gardner, an American developmental psychologist describes 'Intelligence' in various forms as follows:

1. **Linguistic Intelligence:** The ability to speak, recognize, and use tools of phonology (speech sounds), syntax (grammar), and semantics (meaning). Examples of Linguistic Intelligence are Narrators, Orators. These people can by and large, show and express their intelligence through their speech.
2. **Musical Intelligence:** The ability to create, communicate with, and understand meanings made of sound, understanding of pitch, also more importantly rhythm. Example of Musical Intelligence are Musicians, Singers, Composers.
3. **Logical-mathematical Intelligence:** The ability of use and understand complex , abstract ideas and relationships in the absence of any action or objects. Example of Logical; mathematical

intelligence are Mathematicians, Scientists.

4. **Spatial Intelligence:** The ability to perceive visual or spatial information, change it, and re-create visual images ,construct 3D images, and to simply move and rotate images. Examples of Spatial intelligence are Map readers, Astronauts, Physicists.

5. **Bodily-Kinesthetic Intelligence:** The ability to use complete or part of the body to solve problems and control the core, fine and coarse motor skills. Example of Bodily-Kinesthetic intelligence are Players, Dancers.

6. **Intra-personal Intelligence:** The ability to distinguish among one's own emotions, intentions, and motivations. Examples of Intra-personal intelligence are the people such as Gautam Buddha.

7. **Interpersonal Intelligence:** The ability to recognize and make distinctions among other people's feelings, beliefs, and also intentions. Examples of Interpersonal intelligence are Mass Communicators, Interviewers.

8. **Naturalist intelligence:** It refers to the ability to read and understand nature. Having sensitivity towards the non-living elements of all living things is considered "nature smart". Example of naturalist intelligence include botanist, oceanographer, camp counsellor, scout troop leader, gardener, astronomer, meteorologist, geologist or even the landscape architect.

9. **Existential intelligence:** It refers to deep sensitivity and people's ability to handle deep questions such as the meaning of existence. It is one of the most complex of the nine types of intelligence as mentioned by Gardner's research. People with existential intelligence are not only comfortable talking about these serious questions but also strive to find the answer. Examples of existential intelligence include inspirational speaker, writer, clergy, author, philosopher, economist or blogger.

Treasure Link
9 types of Intelligence in Action
Scan QR Code

Scooby-Doo Quest

Q. Find the intelligence related to the names given below:

1. Blogger: __________
2. Chef: __________
3. Operator: __________
4. Astronauts: __________
5. Dancer: __________

Answers. 1. Existential Intelligence **2.** Naturalistic Intelligence **3.** Linguistic Intelligence **4.** Spatial Intelligence **5.** Bodily Kinesthetic Intelligence

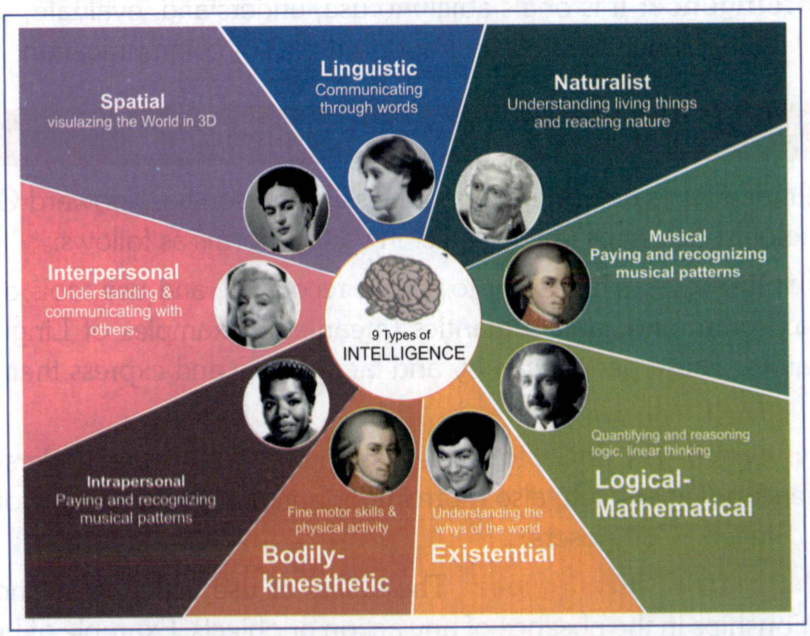

A machine is said to be artificially intelligent , if we develop a machine that has any of the intelligence discussed above. Let us now know the basic difference between natural /human and artificial/ machine intelligence.

FUN.AI ACTIVITY

https://studio.code.org/s/oceans/lessons/1/levels/2

Treasure Link
How AI Works? in Action

Scan QR Code

1. See the magic of AI and listen to the video first.

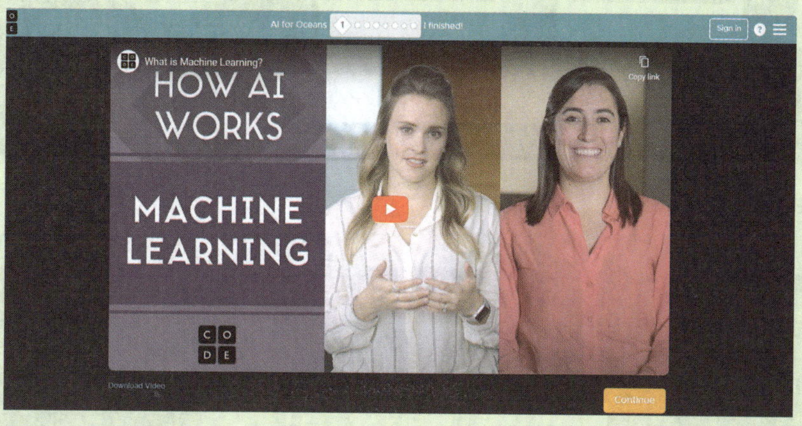

2. Click 'Continue'.

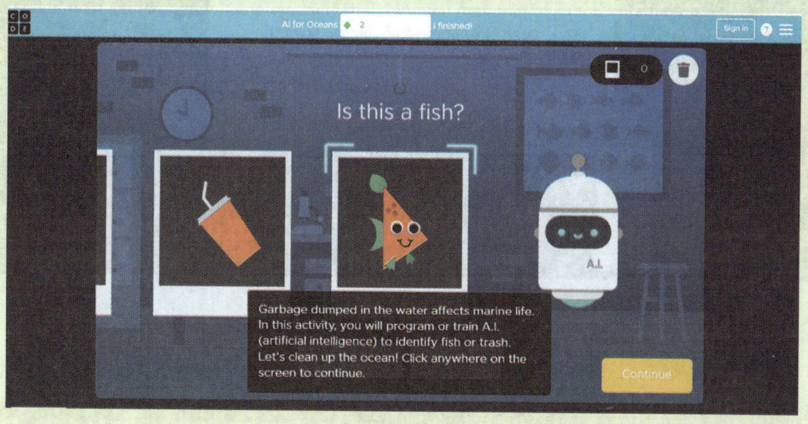

3. Click 'Continue'.

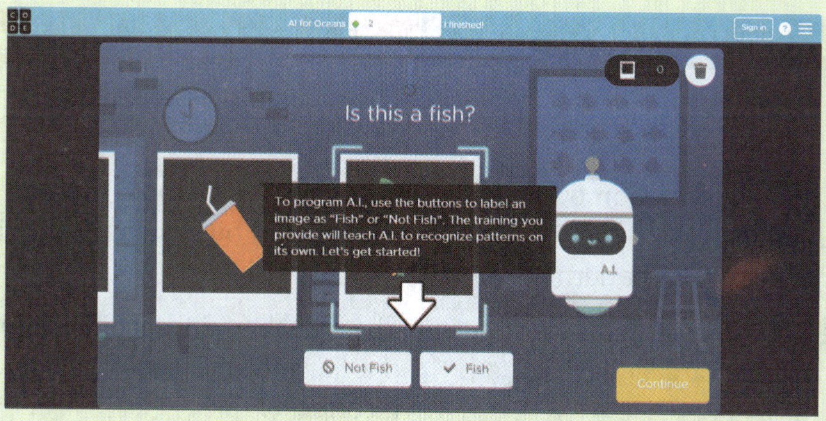

4. Select 'Fish' or 'Not fish' by looking at the picture.

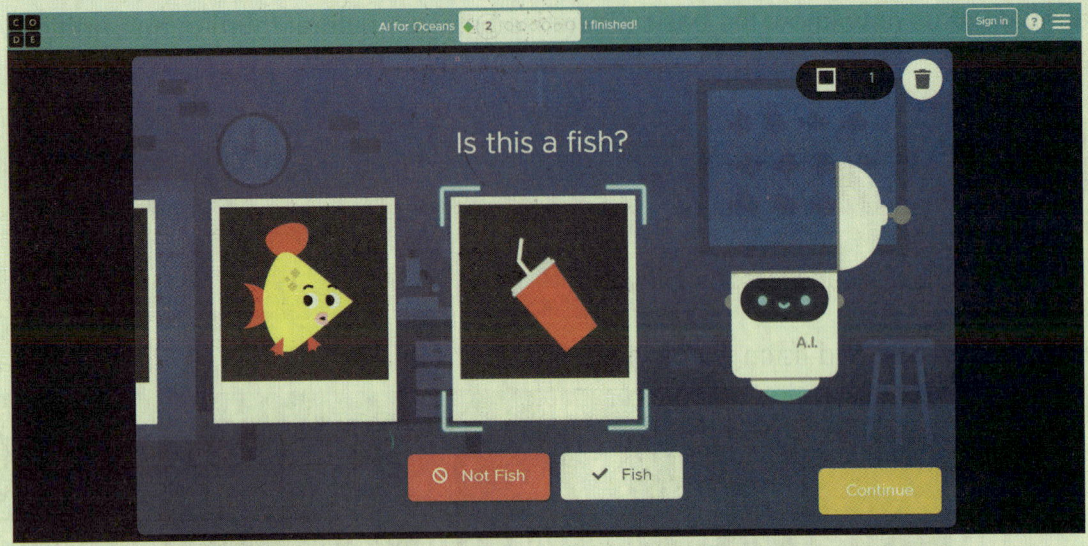

5. It will also give you tips like:

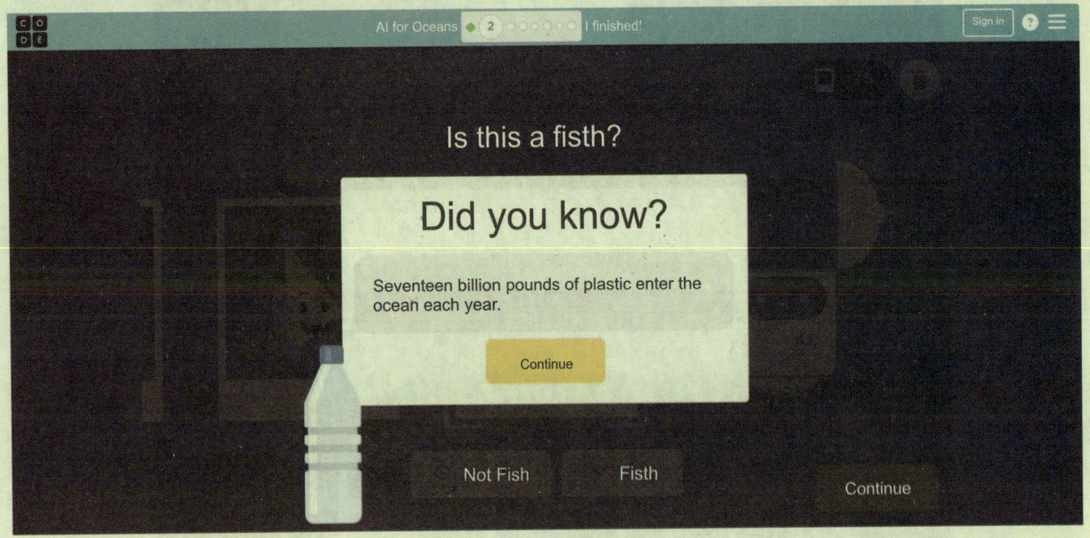

Keep Playing !!!

1.4 DIFFERENCE BETWEEN HUMAN AND THE MACHINE INTELLIGENCE

Human Intelligence	Machine Intelligence
Humans recognise by patterns.	The machines essentially recognize by set of rules and data.
Humans store and recall information by patterns. For example, the number 40404040 is easy to remember, store, and recall as its pattern is simple.	Machines has memory that can store and recall the information by searching algorithms.
Humans can figure out the complete object even if some part of it is missing or even is distorted.	The machines finds it difficult to complete or figure out the missing part of an object and cannot do it correctly.

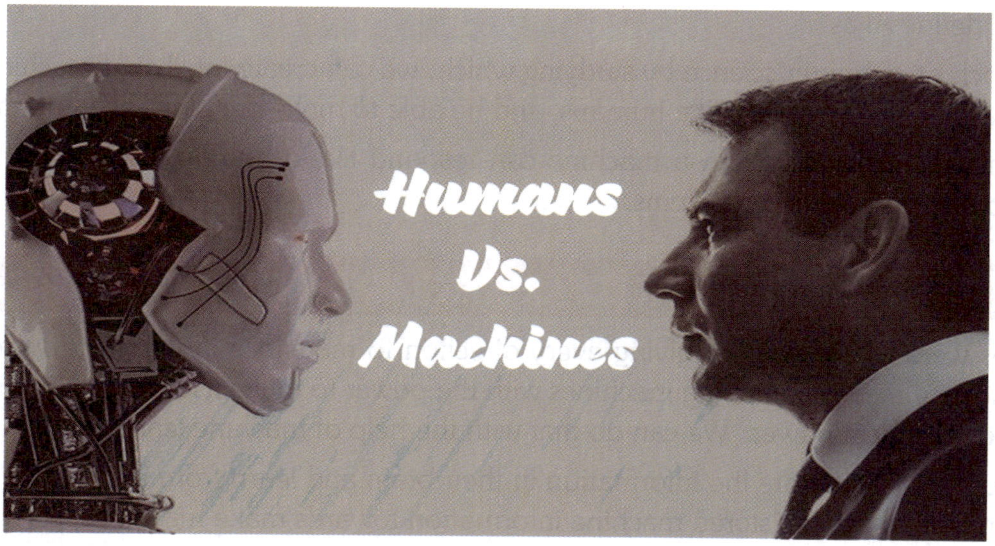

1.5 WHAT IS ARTIFICIAL INTELLIGENCE?

In today's world, technology is growing very fast and we are heading towards one of the flourishing technologies of computer science. This basically refers to Artificial Intelligence which makes a machine as intelligent as a human being. Artificial Intelligence these days is growing around us at a very fast pace. It is currently working in many areas, ranging from general to specific, such as displaying our shopping habits, self-driving cars, playing chess, proving theorems, playing music, even drawing painting, etc.

Treasure Link
What is Artificial Intelligence? in Action

Scan QR Code

Our future lies in AI as humans are looking for devices that can take decision and solve the problems. When a machine displays attributes like learning, reasoning and solving problems that are based on the situation or the environment around, the machine is based on Artificial intelligence.

1.6 UNDERSTANDING ARTIFICIAL INTELLIGENCE

Artificial Intelligence is made up of two words **Artificial** and **Intelligence**, where Artificial means "*man-made*", and intelligence means "*ability to understand and think*", hence AI essentially means "*a man-made ability to understand and think*".

So, we can define AI as:

"It is a branch of computer science by studying which, we can create intelligent machines which can act like a human, think and reason like humans, and be able to make decisions like humans".

Artificial Intelligence exists when a machine can respond like a human displaying the apt skill of learning, reasoning, and solving problems.

1.7 WHY WE NEED ARTIFICIAL INTELLIGENCE?

Human Beings were responsible for giving every direction to machines in the past, but not anymore. Artificial Intelligence means equipping machines with the power to make its own decision like in human beings. How to give them power? We can do that with the help of machine learning.

Just like human beings store the information in their brain and learn from its patterns, the scientists have also been able to use the stored machine information towards make machines learn from them.

For instance, human beings know that fishes swim on the water by storing "fish" in their brain and watching them float on the water over and over again. Likewise, machines can also do the same function by analysing the patterns from their stored information (Machine Learning) and coming out with the conclusion to make decisions like human beings (Artificial Intelligence).

Artificial Intelligence is an approach or skill that can make a computer, a robot, or a product to think how similarly like a human. AI is a study of how human brain think, learn, decide and work, while trying to solve a set of problems. And later this study gives outputs as intelligent software systems. The aim of AI is to improve computer functions which are related to the knowledge of humans , for example, reasoning, learning, and problem-solving.

The long-term goals of the general intelligence sector are to do research in the field of AI related to reasoning, knowledge representation, planning, learning, natural language processing, realization, and also the core ability to move and manipulate objects.

Before Learning about Artificial Intelligence, we should know that what is the importance of AI and why should we learn it. Let us now understand some main reasons that shows the importance of AI:

- With the help of AI, we can create such software or devices which can solve real-world problems easily and with utmost accuracy such as in health issues, marketing, traffic issues, etc.
- With the help of AI, we can create your personal virtual Assistant, like with Cortana, Google Assistant, Siri, etc.
- With the help of AI, we can build such Robots which can work in an environment where the basic survival of humans can be at risk like freezing zones, political boundaries, risky terrain, etc.

Thus we can say that AI opens a new path for other new technologies, new devices, and also new Opportunities for human being.

Scooby-Doo Quest

Q. Find any 3 names of AI Assistant

________, ________ & ________

Ans. Apple Siri, Google Assistant, Amazon Alexa

FUN.AI ACTIVITY

Treasure Link
Quick Draw in Action
Scan QR Code

Visit Quick draw and enjoy the AI Game: https://quickdraw.withgoogle.com/

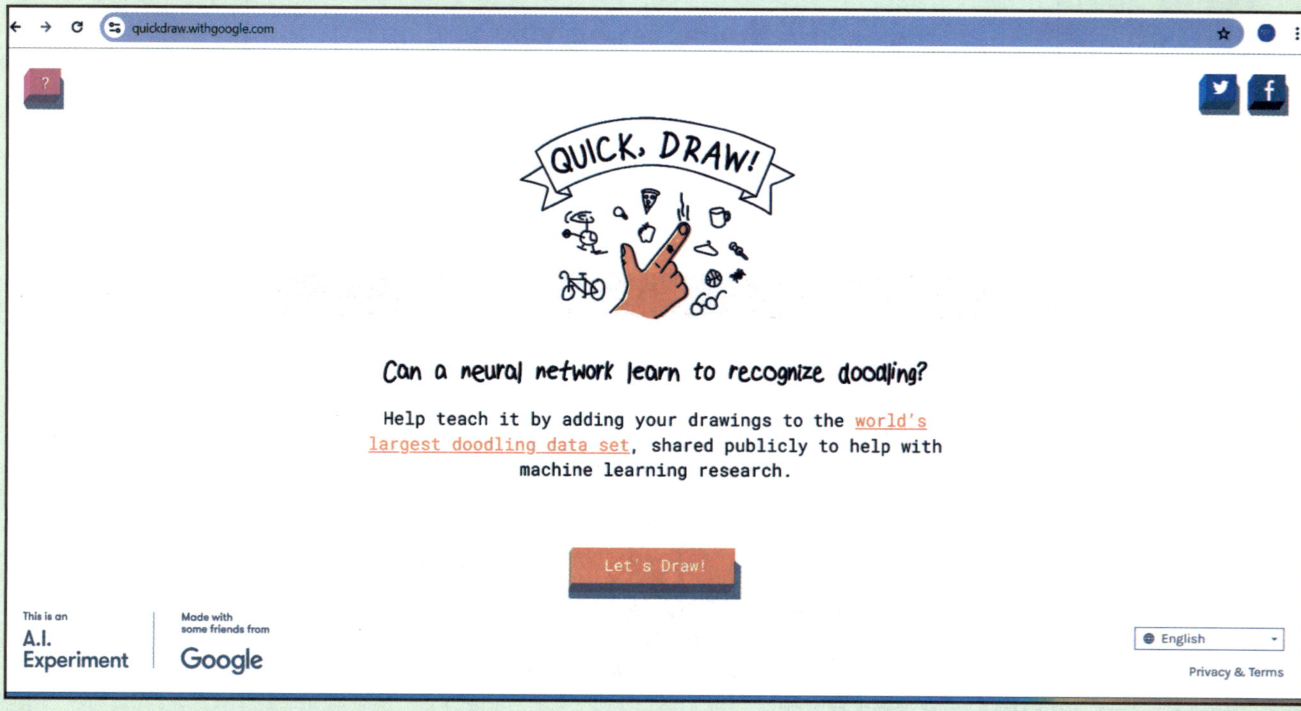

1. Click on "Let's Draw".

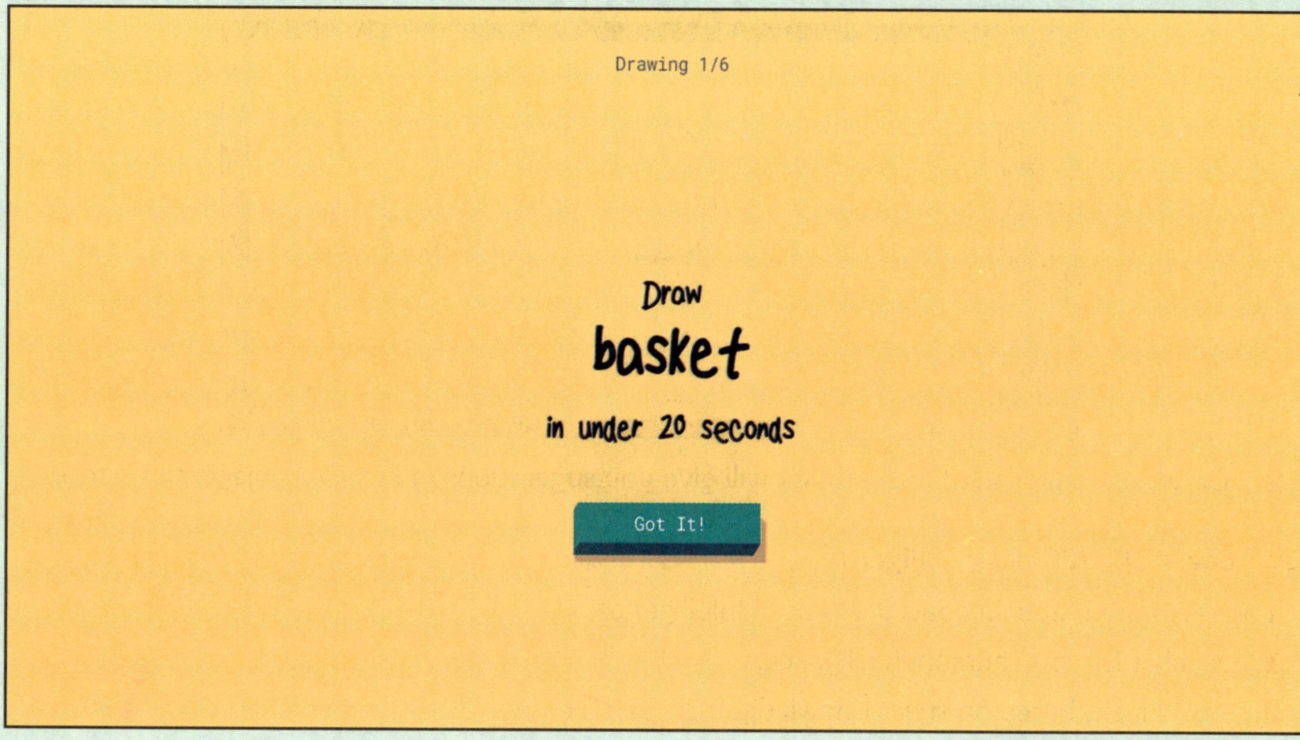

2. Click on 'got it!' You draw the picture and it will tell you whether it is correct or not.

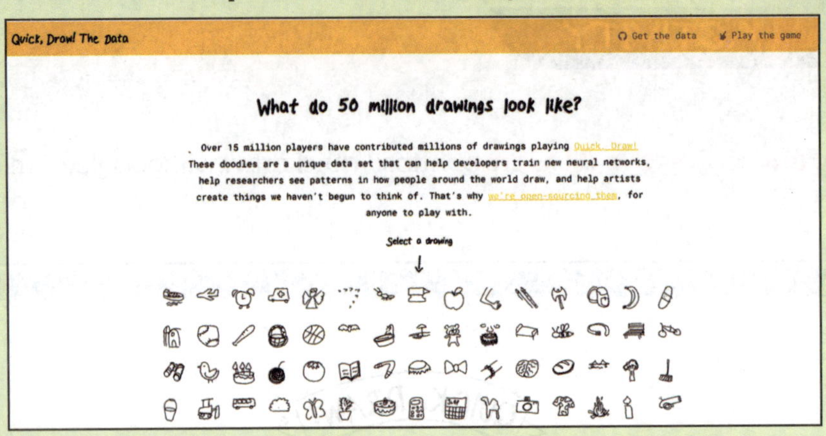

Now start with Autodraw: https://experiments.withgoogle.com/autodraw

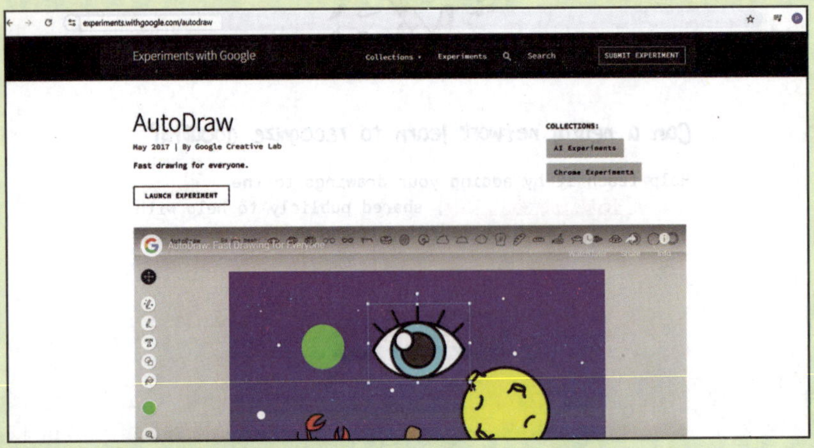

Treasure Link
Autodraw
in Action

Scan QR Code

1. Click on 'LAUNCH EXPERIMENT'.

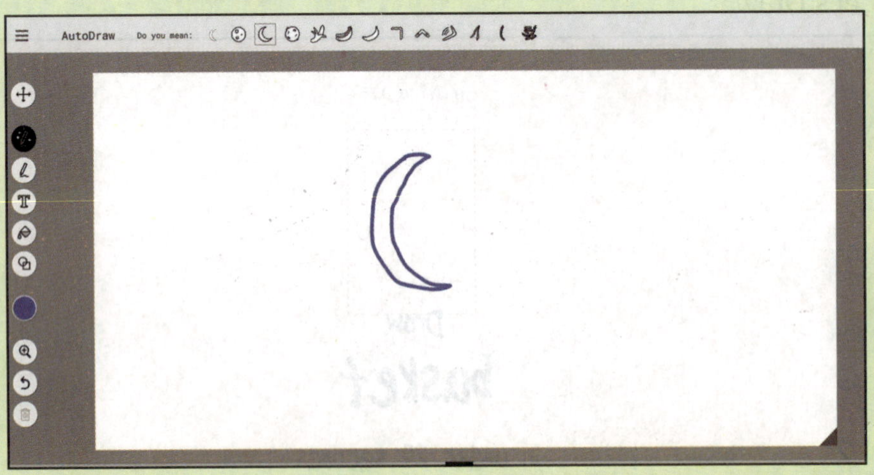

2. Draw something and the computer will give you suggestions of possible objects at the top.

1.7.1 Goals of Artificial Intelligence

Following are the main goals of Artificial Intelligence:

1. Mimic (copying) human intelligence.
2. Solve tasks based on sheer Knowledge.
3. An intelligent connection of observation and also action.

4. Building a machine or a device which can perform tasks that requires human intelligence such as:
   - Proving a theorem.
   - Playing chess.
   - Plan some surgical operation.
   - Driving a car in traffic.
   - Interpreting your language.
5. Creating some system which can truly demonstrate intelligent behavior, learn new things by itself, show, explain, and can advise to its user.

Treasure Link
Artificial Intelligence in Action
Scan QR Code

1.8 HOW IS ARTIFICIAL INTELLIGENCE DIFFERENCE FROM AUTOMATION?

Feature	Automation	Artificial Intelligence (AI)
Meaning	Using machines or computers to do repeated tasks automatically without any human help.	Making machines or computers think, learn, and then make decisions like humans.
Suitable for	Simple, routine, and fixed jobs.	Complex problems wherein the machine must learn and improve.
Example of Task	Printing bills, turning lights on/off at a fixed time.	Chatbots like Alexa/Siri, self-driving cars, Google Translate.
Decision Making	Follows pre-written instructions (cannot change on its own).	Learns from data and all the experience to make better decisions.
Flexibility	It is not flexible as it only does what it is told.	It is Flexible as it can well adapt and improve its answers or actions.
Human-like ability	It doesn't have human abilities as it just follows commands.	It has real abilities like human as it tries to mimic human intelligence.

1.9 ADVANTAGES OF ARTIFICIAL INTELLIGENCE

Some of the advantages of Artificial Intelligence are as follows:

- **AI machines have high accuracy with less errors:** AI machines or systems have high accuracy since it takes decisions as per pre-experience or information. This is why all such systems or machine gives output with less errors.
- **AI machines have high-speed:** AI systems have high-speed and makes fast-decision. An example of this can be seen through the machine that was able to beat a chess champion in the Chess game.

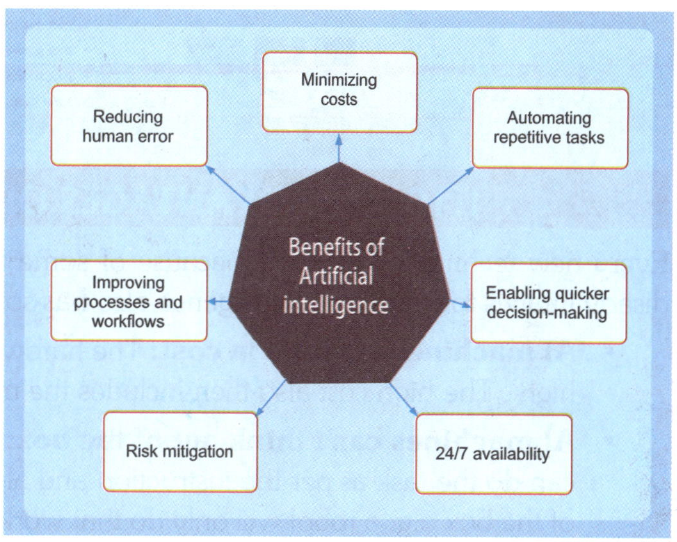

- **AI machines have high reliability:** AI machines are highly reliable and can actually perform the same action multiple times with accuracy.
- **AI machines are best suited for risky areas:** AI machines can be helpful in situations where employing humans can be risky such as defusing a bomb, exploring the ocean floor, keeping an eye on the international border of a country, etc.
- **AI machines can give digital assistant:** AI machines can give digital assistant to the users like it is doing in the field of E-commerce websites for showing the sought products , as per customer requirement.

Scooby-Doo Quest

Q. Find any three things that is a part of Intelligence

1. ________________
2. ________________
3. ________________

Answers: 1. Reasoning **2.** Learning **3.** Problem Solving

- **AI machines can be useful as a public utility:** AI machines can be very useful as public utilities such as a self-driving car for making our journey safer and hassle-free, facial recognition for security purpose, Natural language thereby processing to communicate with the human in human-language, etc.

FUN.AI ACTIVITY

Play ROCK PAPER SCISSORS Game: https://rockpaperscissors-ai.vercel.app/

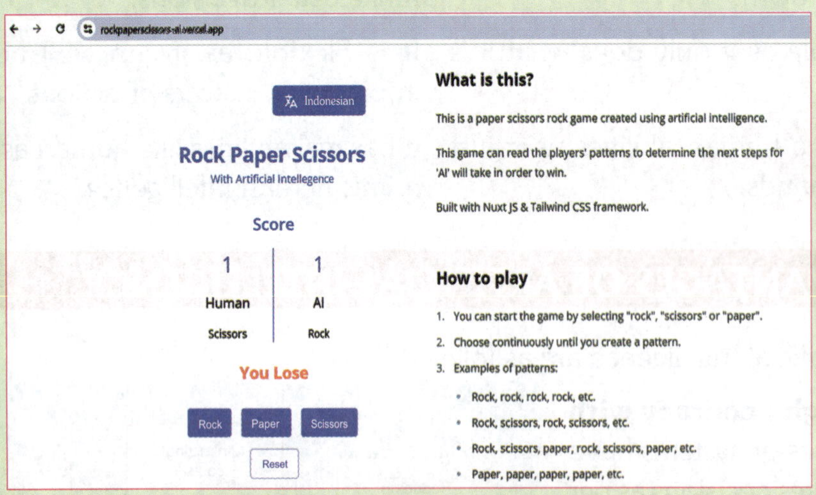

To See Rock Paper Scissor in Action

Scan QR Code

1.10 DISADVANTAGES OF ARTIFICIAL INTELLIGENCE

Every new technology emerges because of some advantages but at the same time it can have some disadvantages too. Artificial Intelligence also has some critical disadvantages:

- **AI machines are high in cost:** The hardware and software requirement of AI machines is quite high . The high cost also then includes the maintenance cost of the AI machines.
- **AI machines can't think out of the box:** With the emergence of AI Technology ,the machines can do the task as per the instruction and algorithm given but still they cannot think or work out of the box e.g. a robot will only do that work for which they are trained or actually programmed.

- **AI machines have no feelings and emotions:** AI machines can only work on the instructions and algorithm given. These machines cannot feel or react so it cannot make any kind of emotional attachment with human, and may even harm all the users if proper care is not taken.
- **AI machines increase human dependency on machines:** AI is a new technology but it has made humans more dependent on the machines or devices and as a result , humans are thereby losing their mental capabilities.
- **AI machines does not have original creativity:** God has blessed humans with intelligence and creativity so humans created the AI machines but on the contrary the AI machines does not have their own intelligence and also, they cannot beat the power of human intelligence and cannot be creative and imaginative.

FUN.AI ACTIVITY

1. **Visit The site:** https://www.neuralframes.com/tools/ai-style-transfer

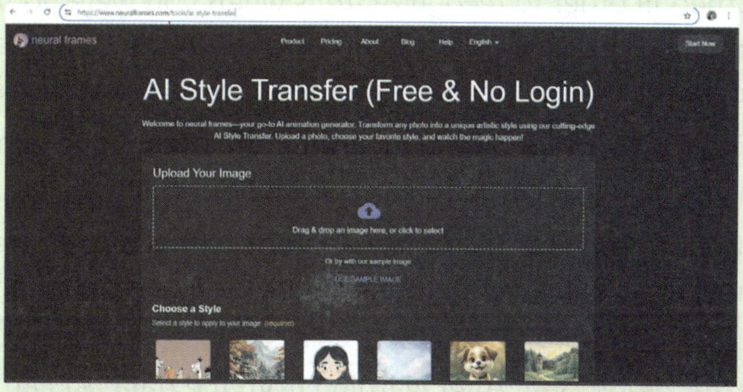

To See Neural Frames in Action

Scan QR Code

2. Drag any image with a pose and then choose the style. Click on a Create styled image. You will see a similar image with the style.

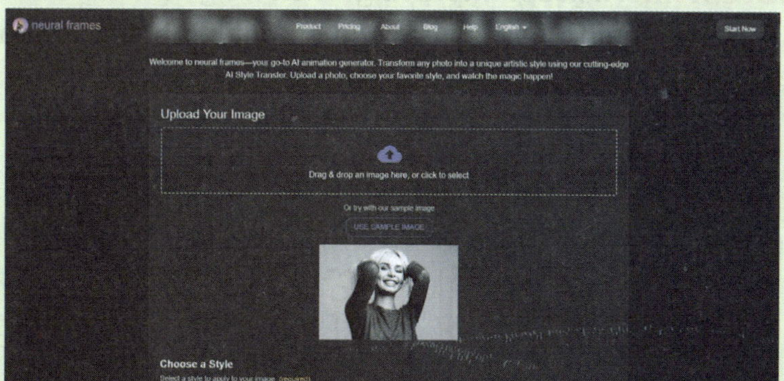

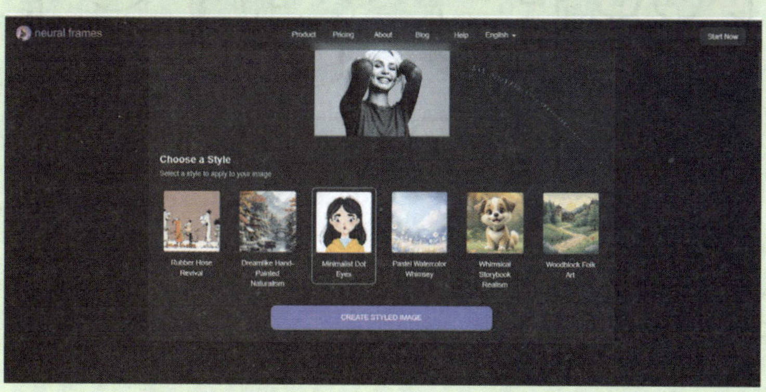

To See
Arbitrary Style Transfer in Action

Scan QR Code

You can also visit another site https://reiinakano.com/arbitrary-image-stylization-tfjs/ to choose Arbitrary Style Transfer in the chosen Browser.

1.11 HOW DOES AI WORK?

Artificial Intelligence, or AI, works in a way that is very similar to how human beings learn new things. Think about how you learned in order to recognize fruits when you were younger. At first, your parents or teachers showed you many pictures of an apple and said, "This is an apple." They repeated it many times until you could recognize an apple on your own. In the same way, AI also learns from examples.

The first step is **giving data to the AI**. Data means information. For example, if we want AI to learn about cats, then we must give it lots of cat pictures. The more pictures it sees, the more it learns.

The second step is **learning patterns**. Just like you notice that apples are usually red or green and round in shape, AI also notices all the given patterns. In the case of cats, it might notice that cats usually have whiskers, two ears, sharp eyes, and four legs.

The third step is **making decisions**. After learning from the data, AI can now use its knowledge to decide what something is. So, if we show AI a new picture of an animal, it can tell whether it is a cat or not.

The last step is **improvement**. AI keeps improving when we give it more data. If AI makes a mistake, then we correct it, and it learns again. This is just like you getting better at maths or cricket when you practice more and more.

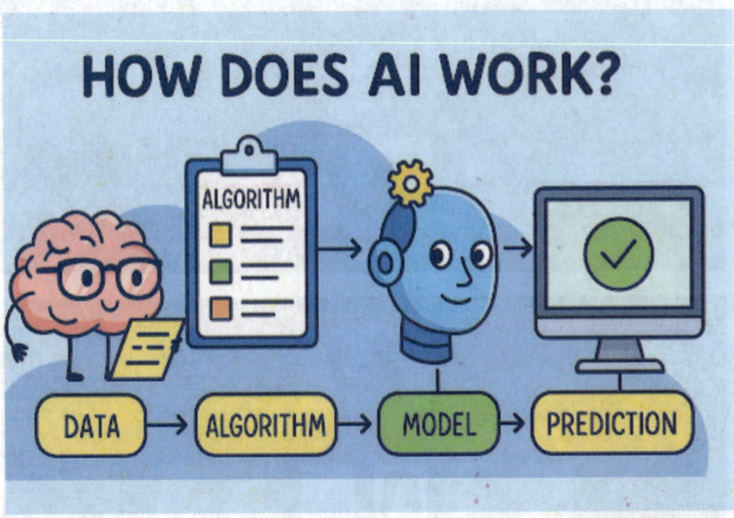

So, in simple words, AI works in four stages: it takes information, learns from it, makes decisions, and tends to improve with practice.

LET'S REHASH

1. **Intelligence** is the ability to think, calculate, reason, and learn from experience, thereby adapting to new situations.
2. Intelligence involves understanding relationships, storing and retrieving information, in the process solving problems, and using language.
3. **Components of intelligence** include reasoning, learning, problem-solving, perception, and also linguistic intelligence.
4. **Reasoning** is the process of making decisions, judging, and of predicting behavior.
5. **Learning** involves gaining knowledge or skills through study, practice, or experience, with different types like auditory and spatial learning.
6. **Problem-solving** is the process of finding solutions to issues by decision-making andv thereby selecting the best alternative.
7. **Perception** involves acquiring, analyzing, interpreting, and also organizing sensory information.
8. **Linguistic intelligence** refers to the ability to use, understand, and to communicate through language.
9. **Types of intelligence** include linguistic, musical, logical-mathematical, spatial, bodily-kinesthetic, intrapersonal, and also interpersonal intelligence.
10. **Machine intelligence** refers to a machine that exhibits any of the types of intelligence discussed.
11. **Human vs. machine intelligence:** Humans recognize patterns, while machines to a large extent, rely on rules and data.
12. **Artificial Intelligence (AI)** is a branch of computer science aimed at creating machines that can act, think, and reason like the human beings.
13. AI is increasingly integrated into areas such as shopping habits, self-driving cars, and playing games.
14. **AI's significance** includes solving real-world problems, creating virtual assistants, and also greatly in developing robots for dangerous environments.
15. **Goals of AI** include mimicking human intelligence, solving knowledge-based tasks, and by building intelligent systems.
16. AI involves disciplines like mathematics, biology, psychology, sociology, and the computer science.
17. **Advantages of AI** include high accuracy, speed, reliability, suitability for risky tasks, digital assistance, and public utility.
18. **Disadvantages of AI** include high cost, lack of creativity, emotional detachment, and all the increased human dependency.
19. AI systems perform tasks based on instructions and cannot think outside the box or exhibit any original creativity.
20. **AI works in four stages:** It takes information, learns from it, makes decisions and thereby improves with practice.

To Solve Multiple Choice Questions Online

Scan QR Code and Check Your Score

EXERCISE

(A) Multiple Choice Questions with Answers

1. What is intelligence primarily about?
(a) Physical strength
(b) Ability to think, calculate, reason, and learn from experience
(c) Ability to run fast
(d) Ability to read and write

2. Which of the following is NOT a type of learning mentioned in the text?
(a) Auditory learning
(b) Spatial learning
(c) Genetic learning
(d) Perceptual learning

3. Reasoning in intelligence involves:
(a) Physical movement
(b) Judging, decision-making, and predicting behaviour
(c) Speaking multiple languages
(d) Eating habits

4. AI machines are best suited for:
(a) Cooking food
(b) Risky areas
(c) Watching movies
(d) Singing songs

5. What is the primary difference between human and machine intelligence?
(a) Machines are slower than humans
(b) Humans recognize things by patterns, while machines use rules and data
(c) Machines can think outside the box
(d) Humans cannot store information

6. Which of the following is NOT a goal of AI?
(a) Mimicking human intelligence
(b) Increasing human dependence
(c) Solving tasks based on knowledge
(d) Creating intelligent systems

7. What type of intelligence involves understanding pitch and rhythm?
(a) Spatial intelligence
(b) Logical-mathematical intelligence
(c) Musical intelligence
(d) Bodily-kinesthetic intelligence

8. AI machines are characterized by:
(a) High creativity
(b) High accuracy and speed
(c) Emotional understanding
(d) Low reliability

9. Which field is NOT directly involved in AI development?
(a) Mathematics
(b) Sociology
(c) Medicine
(d) Computer Science

10. AI machines lack:

(a) Original creativity (b) Memory
(c) Processing power (d) Speed

11. What is a key disadvantage of AI machines?

(a) They are very cheap (b) They have emotions
(c) They increase human dependence (d) They think out of the box

12. In AI, which term describes the ability of a machine to mimic human decision-making?

(a) Robotics (b) Learning
(c) Perception (d) Artificial Intelligence

13. Problem-solving in intelligence involves:

(a) Ignoring issues (b) Finding solutions through decision-making
(c) Creating new problems (d) Listening to music

14. Intrapersonal intelligence refers to:

(a) Understanding others' emotions (b) Understanding one's own emotions
(c) Building physical strength (d) Playing musical instruments

15. What does AI aim to improve in computer functions?

(a) Physical appearance
(b) Knowledge representation, reasoning, and problem-solving
(c) Speed of typing
(d) Internet connectivity

16. AI machines are reliable because:

(a) They can perform the same action multiple times fully accurately
(b) They are expensive
(c) They have human emotions
(d) They seldom make mistakes

17. Linguistic intelligence is primarily about:

(a) Have written command over a language
(b) Understanding and using languages
(c) Being able to speak well
(d) Designing architecture

18. Which of the following is a disadvantage of AI machines?

(a) They are not so creative (b) They have a short life cycle
(c) They lack emotions (d) They abuse human intelligence

19. Perception in AI is the process of:

(a) Interpreting language (b) Acquiring and interpreting sensory information
(c) Building robots (d) Interpreting to music

20. The term "Artificial" in Artificial Intelligence means:

(a) Natural (b) Man-made
(c) Creative (d) Emotional

ANSWERS

1.	(b)	2.	(c)	3.	(b)	4.	(b)	5.	(b)
6.	(b)	7.	(c)	8.	(b)	9.	(c)	10.	(a)
11.	(c)	12.	(d)	13.	(b)	14.	(b)	15.	(b)
16.	(a)	17.	(b)	18.	(c)	19.	(b)	20.	(b)

(B) Fill in the Blanks with Answers

1. __________ is the basic ability to think, calculate, reason, and learn from experience.

Ans. Intelligence

2. __________ generally involves judging, decision-making, and predicting behavior.

Ans. Reasoning

3. __________ is the clear process of gaining knowledge or skill by studying, practicing, or experiencing.

Ans. Learning

4. __________ is essentially finding solutions through decision-making.

Ans. Problem-solving

5. __________ involves acquiring, analyzing, interpreting, and also organizing sensory information.

Ans. Perception

6. __________ commonly refers to the ability to understand and use language.

Ans. Linguistic intelligence

7. __________ is a basic branch of computer science aimed at creating intelligent machines.

Ans. Artificial Intelligence

8. AI aims to mimic human __________ and to solve tasks based on knowledge.

Ans. intelligence

9. __________ enables all machines to learn from stored information.

Ans. Machine learning

10. __________ machines are generally highly reliable and can perform the same action accurately multiple times.

Ans. AI

11. AI machines have high __________ and speed in decision-making.

Ans. accuracy

12. __________ described intelligence in various forms like linguistic and musical intelligence.

Ans. Howard Gardner

13. __________ intelligence is the ability to understand complex abstract ideas.

Ans. Logical-mathematical

14. AI machines are best suited for __________ areas wherein human survival may be difficult.

Ans. risky

15. AI machines lack __________ and thus they cannot make emotional connections with humans.

Ans. emotions

(c) Short Questions with Answers

1. How is intelligence define?

Ans. Intelligence is the basic ability to think, calculate, reason, learn from experience, solve problems, and adapt to new situations.

2. What are the main components of intelligence?

Ans. The main components of intelligence involve reasoning, learning, problem-solving, perception, and linguistic intelligence.

3. What is the difference between human and machine intelligence?

Ans. Human intelligence clearly recognizes patterns and stores information naturally, while machine intelligence relies on rules, data, and algorithms.

4. What is Artificial Intelligence (AI)?

Ans. Artificial Intelligence is a root branch of computer science focused on creating machines that can think, reason, and act like humans.

5. Why do we need Artificial Intelligence?

Ans. We need Artificial Intelligence in order to create machines that can make decisions, solve problems, and perform tasks that require human intelligence, improving efficiency and handling complex tasks.

6. What are the key advantages of AI machines?

Ans. AI machines offer high accuracy, speed, reliability, suitability for risky tasks, digital assistance, and utility in public services.

7. What are the disadvantages of AI machines?

Ans. AI machines have high costs, lack creativity, emotions, and increase human dependency on technology.

8. What is the role of reasoning in intelligence?

Ans. Reasoning is the process of making decisions, judging, and predicting behaviour based on logic and understanding.

9. What is linguistic intelligence?

Ans. Linguistic intelligence is the core ability to use, understand, and communicate effectively through verbal and written language.

10. How does AI differ from any traditional computing?

Ans. AI differs from traditional computing by enabling machines to learn from data, reason, and make decisions, mimicking human intelligence.

ACTIVITY-BASED QUESTIONS

1. **Activity:** Draw a chart to show various types of Intelligence with examples.
2. **Activity:** Create a detailed collage to show advantages of AI.

TEACHER'S NOTES

1.1 Introduction about Intelligence

- Intelligence = ability to think, reason, learn, and adapt.

Activity: Ask a riddle and discuss how students used thinking to solve it.

1.2 What is Intelligence Made of

- Components: Reasoning, Learning, Problem-Solving, Perception, Linguistic ability.

Activity: Group students—each explains one component with a daily-life example.

1.3 Types of Intelligence

- Nine types by Howard Gardner (linguistic → existential).

Activity: Students identify which type suits them and share examples.

1.4 Human vs Machine Intelligence

- Humans learn by patterns; machines follow data and algorithms.

Activity: Show a half image and ask students to guess the object (humans fill gaps easily).

1.5 What is AI

- AI = Machine's ability to think and act like humans.

Activity: Demonstrate a chatbot or voice assistant and discuss how it "thinks".

1.6 Understanding AI

- "Artificial" = man-made; "Intelligence" = thinking power.

Activity: Write the word "AI" on board – ask students to list where they have seen it used.

1.7 Why We Need AI

- Solves real-world problems, works in risky areas, helps in decision-making.

Activity: Brainstorm: "How can AI help at school or home?"

1.8 AI vs Automation

- Automation = fixed tasks; AI = learns and improves.

Activity: Compare washing machine (automation) vs Alexa (AI).

1.9 Advantages of AI

- High accuracy, speed, safety, reliability.

Activity: Create a "Pros of AI" chart on board with student ideas.

1.10 Disadvantages of AI

- Costly, no emotions, less creativity, human dependency.

Activity: Hold a short class debate: "Can AI replace humans?"

1.11 How AI Works

- Four steps: Takes data → Learns patterns → Makes decisions → Improves.

Activity: Show pictures of cats/dogs; students "train" themselves to identify cats—simulate AI learning.

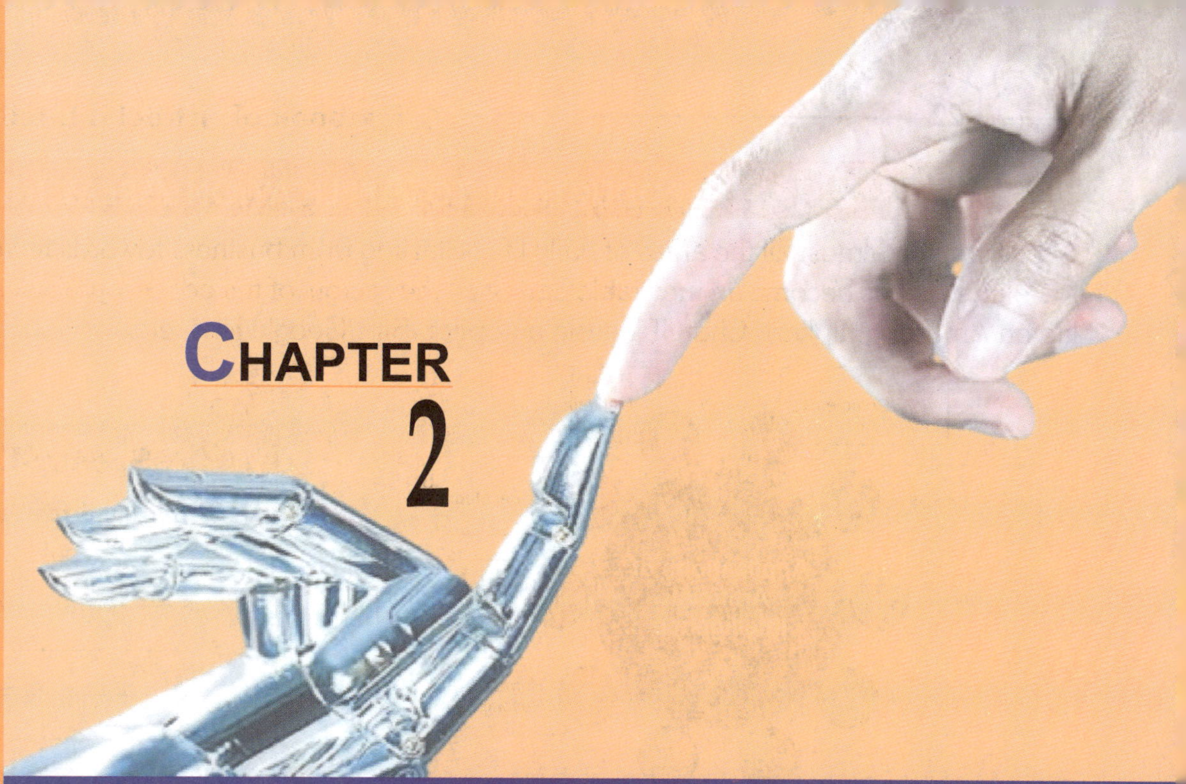

CHAPTER 2

APPLICATION AREAS OF AI

Application Areas of AI
in Action

Scan QR Code

OBJECTIVES

TOPICS TO BE COVERED

- Introduction to Application areas in AI
- Real Life Applications of Research Areas
- Application of AI
- Real Life Application Names

2.1 Introduction to Application Areas in AI

AI has crept in almost all the areas of daily life . Starting from business towards recreation and education to Politics, AI has become an inevitable part of all the sectors of the economy. You can find AI in our daily life on Amazon , flipkart, ChatGPT, tesla autopilot, Siri, Google lens, etc.

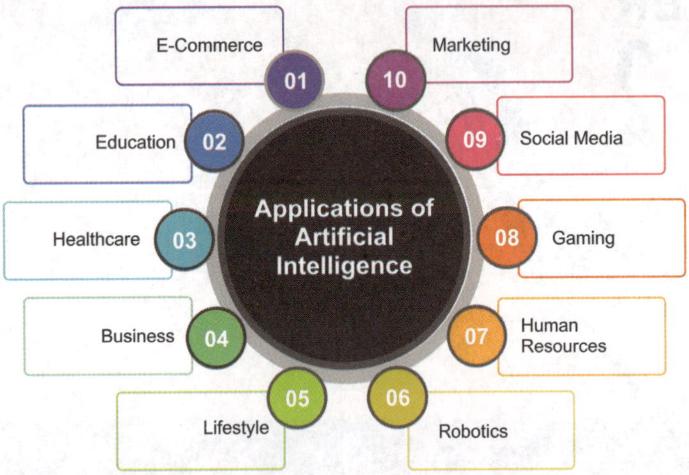

Scooby-Doo Quest

Q. Write any 5 task a ROBOT can do:

1. ____________
2. ____________
3. ____________
4. ____________
5. ____________

Answers: 1. Cleaning floor **2.** Operation **3.** Gardening **4.** Painting **5.** Cooking food

2.2 Real Life Applications of Research Areas

The domain of artificial intelligence is large and widespread. The broadly common and most prospering research areas in the domain of AI are as follows:

Sr.No.	Research Areas
1.	**Expert Systems:** Related to those devices that can either be trained for working as humans, or fully replaced them **Examples:** Flight-tracking systems, Clinical systems.
2.	**Natural Language Processing:** Related to those core devices that use human language for operating. **Examples:** Google Now feature, speech recognition, Automatic voice output.
3.	**Neural Networks:** Related to those core devices that work the way human brain neurons work . **Examples:** Pattern recognition systems such as face recognition, character recognition, handwriting recognition.
4.	**Robotics:** Related to those devices that are programmed to do a task in a factory or an industry. **Examples:** Industrial robots for moving, spraying, painting, precision checking, drilling, cleaning, coating, carving, etc.
5.	**Fuzzy Logic Systems:** Related to those devices that are based on human reasoning . **Examples:** Consumer electronics, automobiles, etc.

2.3 Application of AI

AI or artificial intelligence can simplybe understood as simulating human intelligence processes by machines, especially computer systems. These processes include learning, reasoning and self-correction.

AI was coined by **John McCarthy**, an American computer scientist, in 1956 at The Dartmouth Conference. This term that explains everything from robotic process automation to actual robotics. AI can perform complex tasks like identifying patterns using data more effectively than the humans, enabling deeper view of businesses prospects, analyzing large data for mapping poverty and climate change, automate agricultural practices and irrigation, individualize healthcare and learning, predict consumption patterns, evaluate energy-usage and waste-management.

Treasure Link
2024 AI – 10 Things in Action

Scan QR Code

John McCarthy

- 1955 develop the phrase "Artificial Intelligence"
- 1960 First LISP implementation
- 1971 Turing Award Recipient
- 2001 Conferred the honour of Professor Emeritus of Computer Science at Stanford University

FUN.AI ACTIVITY

Treasure Link
Play Emoji Scavenger in Action

Scan QR Code

Play Emoji Scavenger Hunt: https://emojiscavengerhunt.withgoogle.com/

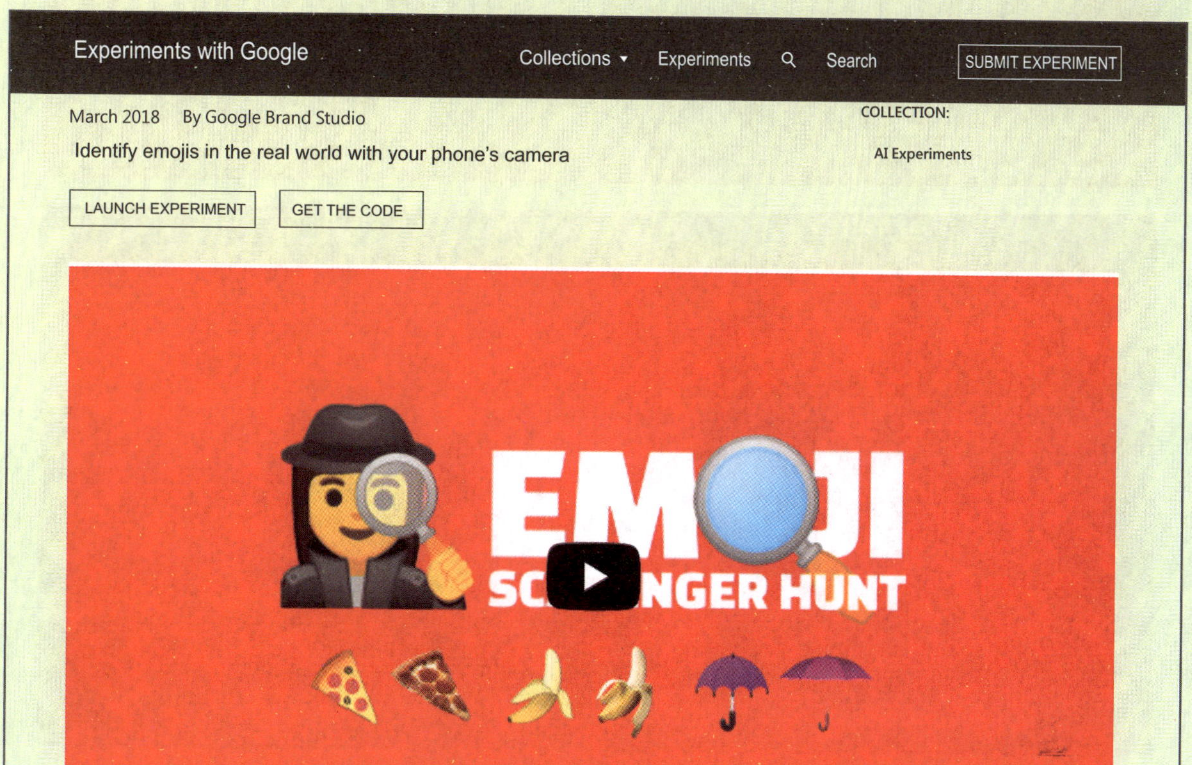

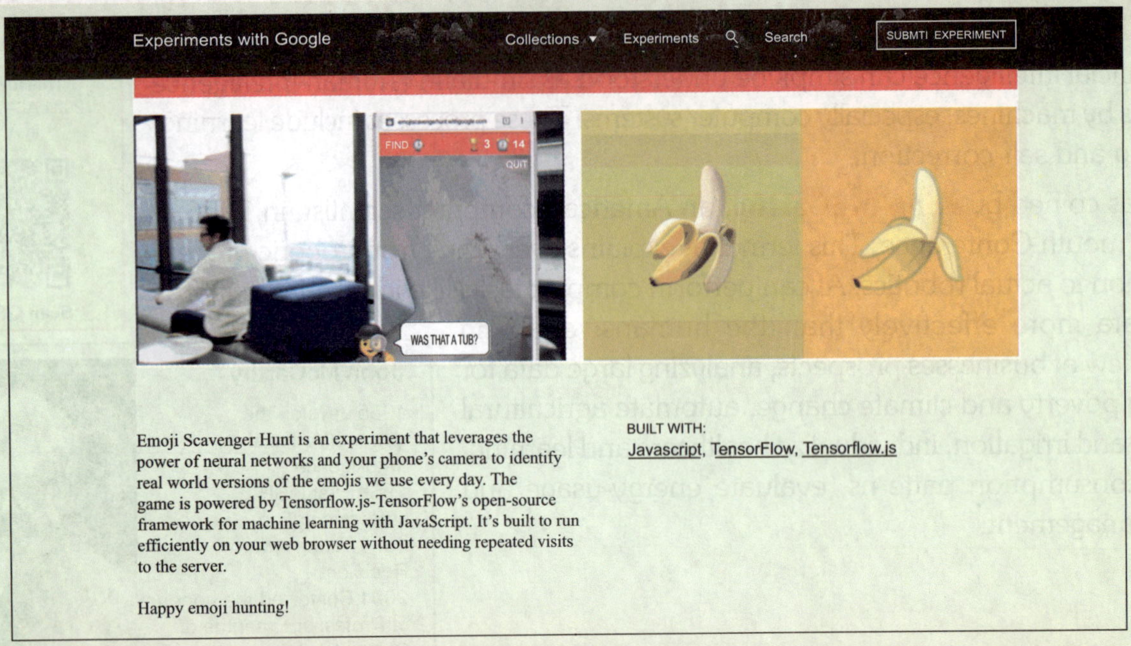
Experiments with Google
Collections
Experiments
Search
SUBMTI EXPERIMENT
FIND
3
14
QUIT
WAS THAT A TUB?
Emoji Scavenger Hunt is an experiment that leverages the power of neural networks and your phone's camera to identify real world versions of the emojis we use every day. The game is powered by Tensorflow.js-TensorFlow's open-source framework for machine learning with JavaScript. It's built to run efficiently on your web browser without needing repeated visits to the server.
Happy emoji hunting!
BUILT WITH:
Javascript, TensorFlow, Tensorflow.js

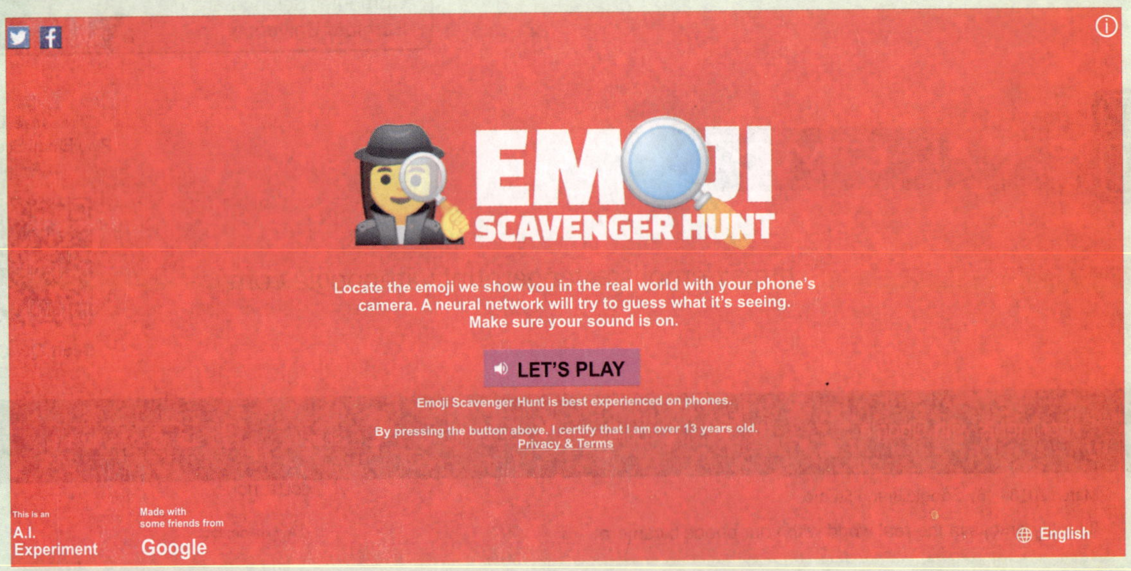
EMOJI
SCAVENGER HUNT
Locate the emoji we show you in the real world with your phone's camera. A neural network will try to guess what it's seeing. Make sure your sound is on.
LET'S PLAY
Emoji Scavenger Hunt is best experienced on phones.
By pressing the button above, I certify that I am over 13 years old.
Privacy & Terms
This is an
A.I.
Experiment
Made with
some friends from
Google
English

3
Find the emoji and point your camera at it before the time expires.

It will ask to find an item. So place the real-life item in front of the camera of your device.

AI is thereby making our daily life more comfortable and easy and that is why artificial Intelligence has various applications in today's world like solving complex problems in an efficient way in many industries, such as Healthcare, entertainment, finance, education, etc. Following are some of the key sectors which have the application of Artificial Intelligence:

Treasure Link
Enjoy and learn AI in Action
Scan QR Code

Treasure Link
Application of AI in Action
Scan QR Code

1. **Astronomy:** Artificial Intelligence can be very useful to solve complex universe problems. AI technology can be useful in understanding our entire universe and how it works. This then implementation could better explain the mankind about the origin of our galaxies and other milky way.

2. **Healthcare:** Healthcare Industries are applying AI to make a better and faster medical diagnosis than humans. AI can help doctors with diagnoses and can thereby inform when the condition of patients are deteriorating so that medical help can reach to the patient before hospitalization. The AI-based applications are useful in understanding medical data and drawing conclusion about the medical health of humans. These applications are applied in various diagnosis and treatment protocol development, drug development, prescribing medicine, and patient monitoring and care.

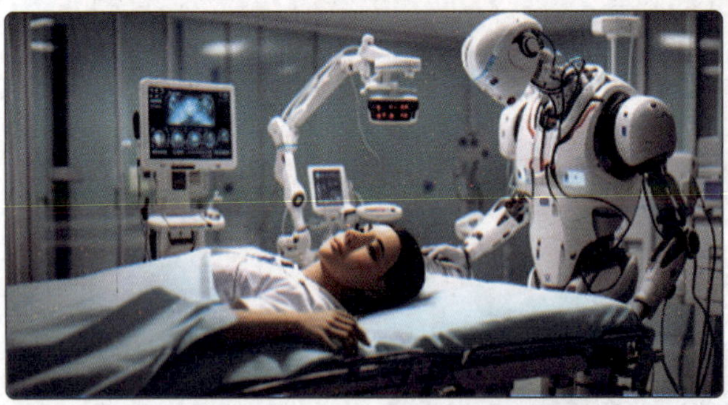

3. **Gaming:** The AI machines can play strategic games like chess, where the machine needs to think of a large number of possible places. Many 3D and online games that are essentially based on AI are also being played which has made games, an industry, these days.

Scooby-Doo Quest

Q. Write any 5 areas where AI is used in Healthcare

1. ____________
2. ____________
3. ____________
4. ____________
5. ____________

Answers: **1.** Diagnosing disease **2.** Prescribe medicine **3.** Patient monitoring **4.** Doing surgery **5.** Manufacturing medicine

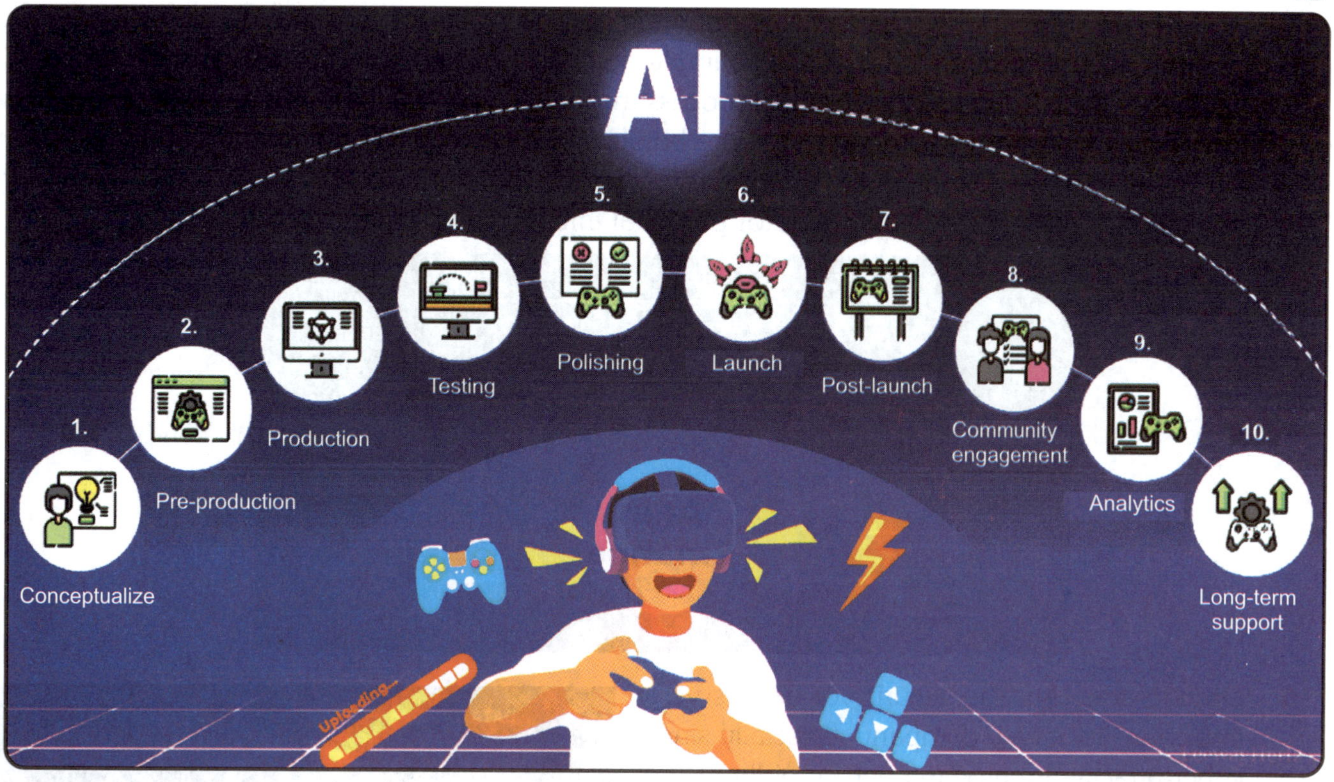

FUN.AI ACTIVITY

Chat with Kuki chatbot and feel as if you are talking to yourself:
https://chat.kuki.ai/chat

Treasure Link
Chat with Kuki Chatbot in Action

Scan QR Code

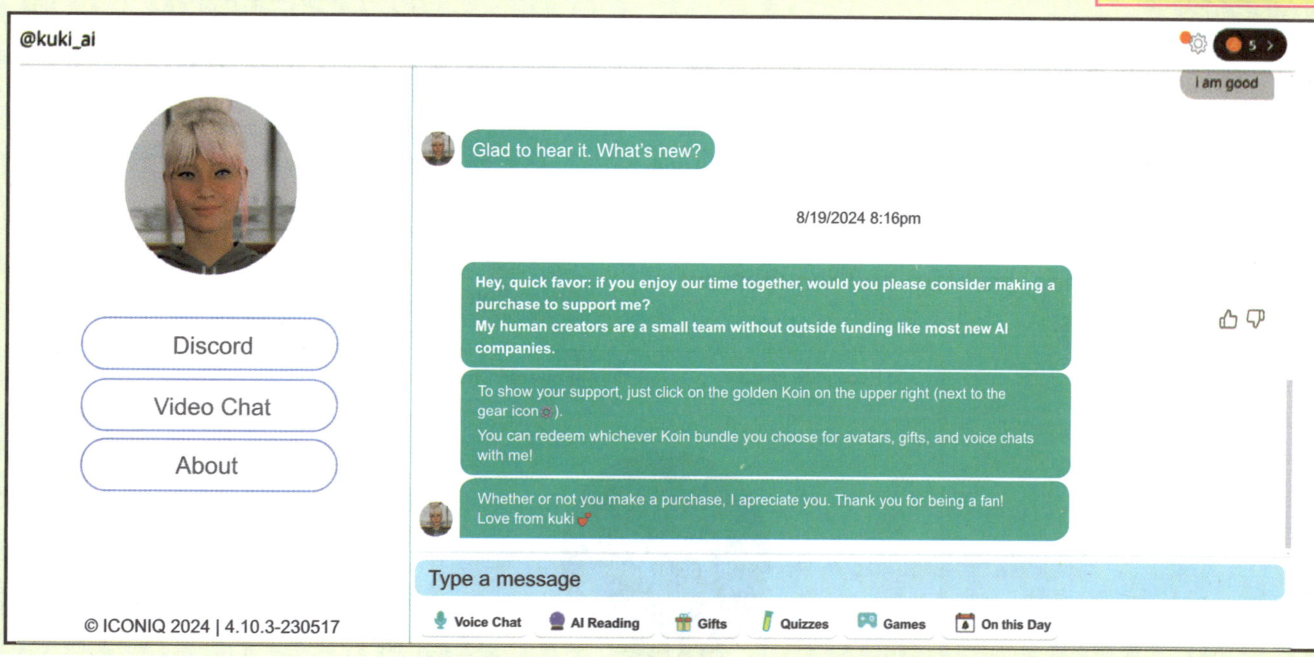

4. **Finance:** The finance industry is implementing automation, chatbot, adaptive intelligence, algorithm trading, and machine learning into financial processes. Many major banks across the

world have thus implemented these emerging technologies for automation and as powerful tools for their effective operations. The implementation of the AI in the banking helped in the payment efforts and reduced complex process through simple chatbots conversation to continue the operations without any hassles. Some banks are also using AI technology in the field of an intelligent virtual assistant, in order to improve their customer services where as some of them are using this to prevent fraud and monitor potential threats to customers in commerce.

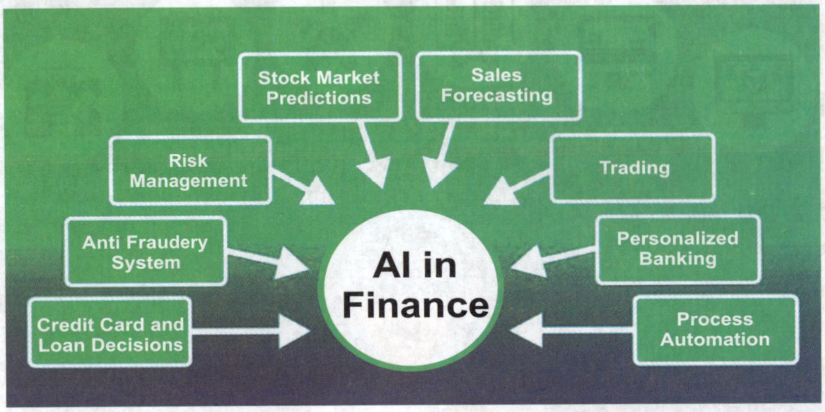

5. **Data Security:** The security of data is very important for every company especially since cyber-attacks are growing very rapidly in the digital world. AI can be used to make the data more safe and secure. Some relevant examples of AI technology are shown in the field of security by AEG bot, AI2 Platform which can determine software bug and cyber-attacks in a better way.

6. **Social Media:** Social Media sites such as Facebook, Twitter, and Snapchat refer to billions of user profiles, which are stored and managed in a very efficient way through the AI Technique. AI can organize, evaluate and effectively manage massive amounts of data to identify the latest trends, hashtag, and requirement of different users.

Scooby-Doo Quest

Q. Write any 3 names of social media sites that has some AI features

1. ________ 2. ________

3. ________ 4. ________

5. ________

Answers: 1. X (Twitter) 2. Facebook 3. Facebook 4. Instagram 5. Snapchat

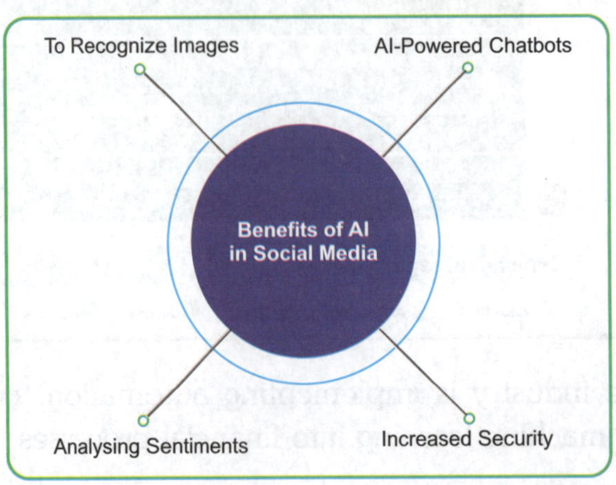

7. **Travel & Transport:** AI is capable of doing various travel related works such as from making travel arrangement to suggesting the hotels, flights, and its best routes to the customers. Travel industries are using AI-enabled chatbots which can make human-like interaction with customers for better and fast response.

8. **Automotive Industry:** Some Automotive industries are using AI to provide virtual assistant to their customers for better performance. One of the famous examples of AI in automation industry is TeslaBot, an intelligent virtual assistant introduced by Tesla. Various Automotive Industries are also currently working consistently, on developing self-driven cars which can make your journey more safe and secure.

9. **Robotics:** Artificial Intelligence has a major role in Robotics. Usually, general robots are programmed such that they can perform some repetitive task, but with the help of AI, we can create intelligent robots which can perform tasks with their own experiences without pre-programmed. Humanoid Robots are thereby the best examples for AI in robotics, recently the intelligent Humanoid robot named as Erica and Sophia has been developed which can talk and behave like humans.

10. **Entertainment:** In the field of Entertainment , we are now using some AI based applications in our daily life such as Netflix or Amazon Prime. With the help of machine learning algorithms, these services show the recommendations towards programs or shows depending on your search history.

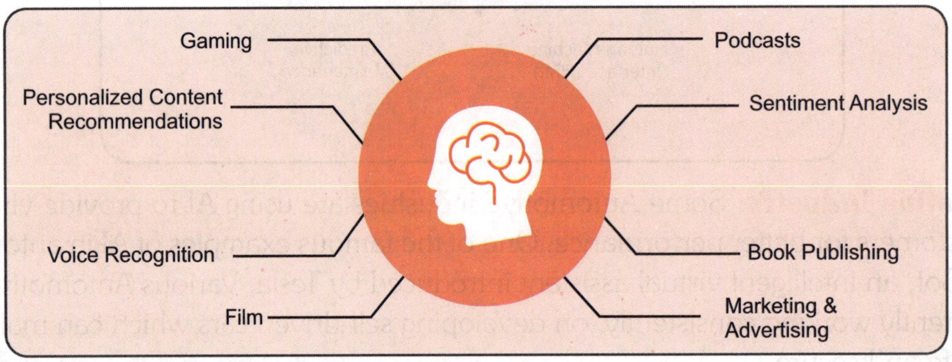

FUN.AI ACTIVITY

Start the Semi-conductor activity and enjoy how you can now become a part of this wonderful Orchestra: https://semiconductor.withgoogle.com/

Treasure Link
Semi-conductor Activity in Action

Scan QR Code

Note: Open this link on desktop for better working.

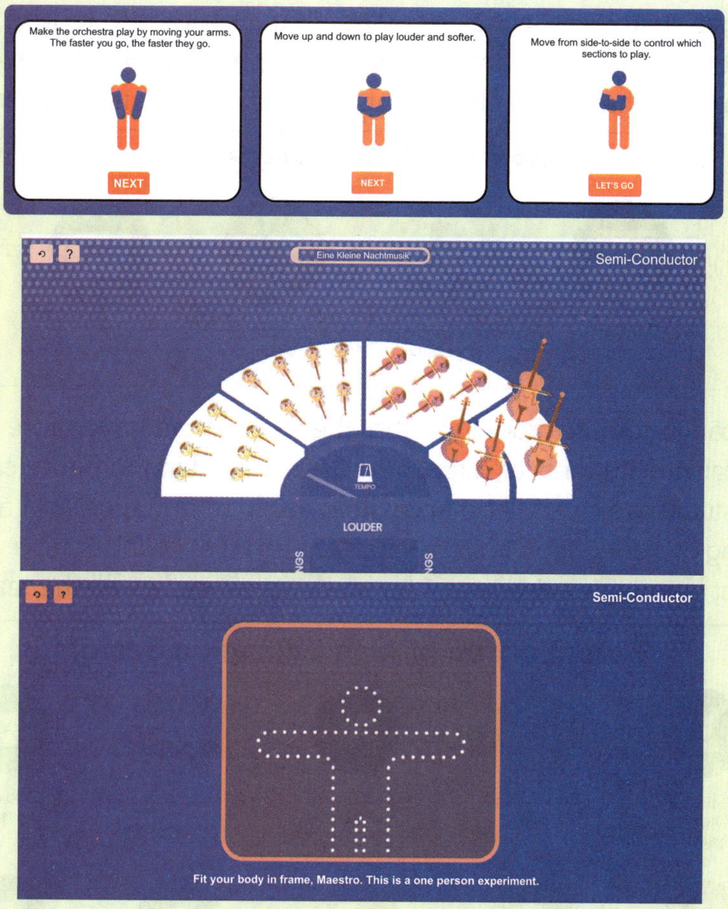

11. Agriculture: Agriculture is now becoming digital, and AI is emerging in this field. Agriculture is applying AI as agriculture robotics, solid and crop monitoring, predictive analysis. AI in agriculture can thereby be very helpful for farmers. Agriculture is one of the core sectors and we have been modifying the cultivation process to yield more from it. The technologies like AI & IoT (Internet of Things) will be very useful in fully understanding a timely planting, getting predictions, using fertilizers, harvesting and the climate.

Treasure Link
How AI Works in Everyday Life
in Action

Scan QR Code

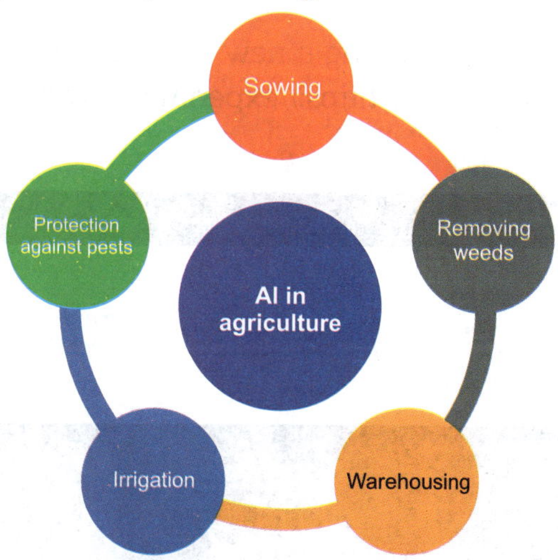

12. E-commerce: AI is helping shoppers to find related products with recommended size, color, or brand. Major e-commerce companies have been using advanced technologies like AI or machine learning by effectively using the AI as chatbots, AI assistants, smart logistics, using algorithms to predict and analyze customers' behaviors. The ultimate aim is to reduce shipping costs. Machine learning helps companies in demand forecasting, product search ranking, product and deals recommendations, merchandising placements, fraud detection, translations and many many more.

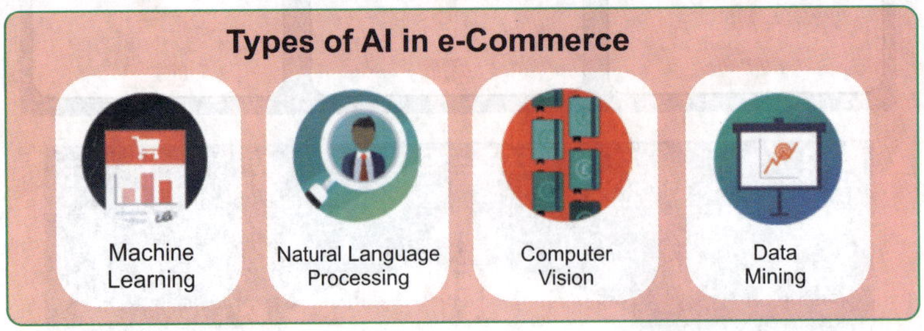

13. **Education:** AI can automate grading so that the teacher can have more time to teach. AI chatbot can communicate with students as a teaching assistant. AI in the future can ably act as a personal virtual tutor for students, who will be accessible easily at any time and any place. AI or machine learning is making our education system smarter and AI & collaborative virtual networks are used to make a perfect learning environment for students as well as all the teachers.

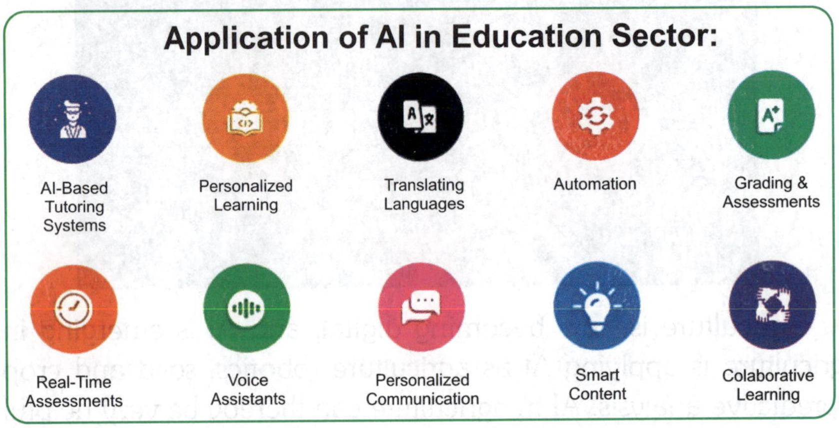

FUN.AI ACTIVITY

Test the limits of computer vision while learning a new language. It is basically a translator for pictures. Requires a camera. https://experiments.withgoogle.com/thing-translator

Treasure Link
Thing Translator in Action

Scan QR Code

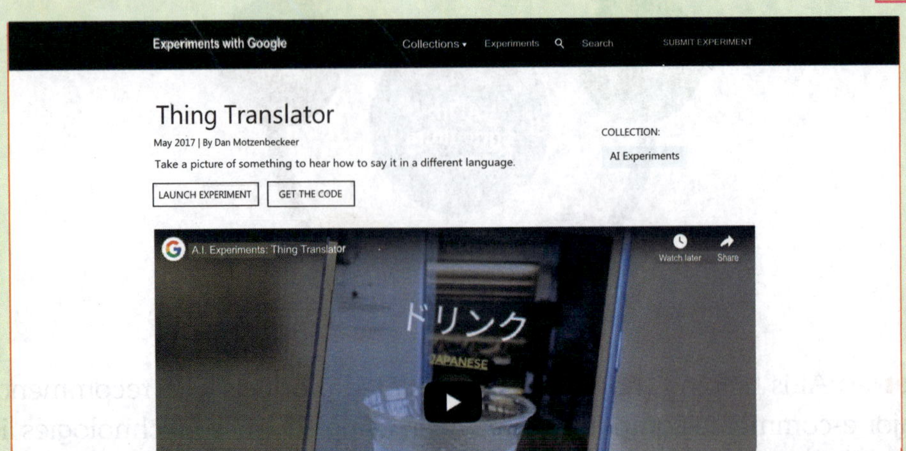

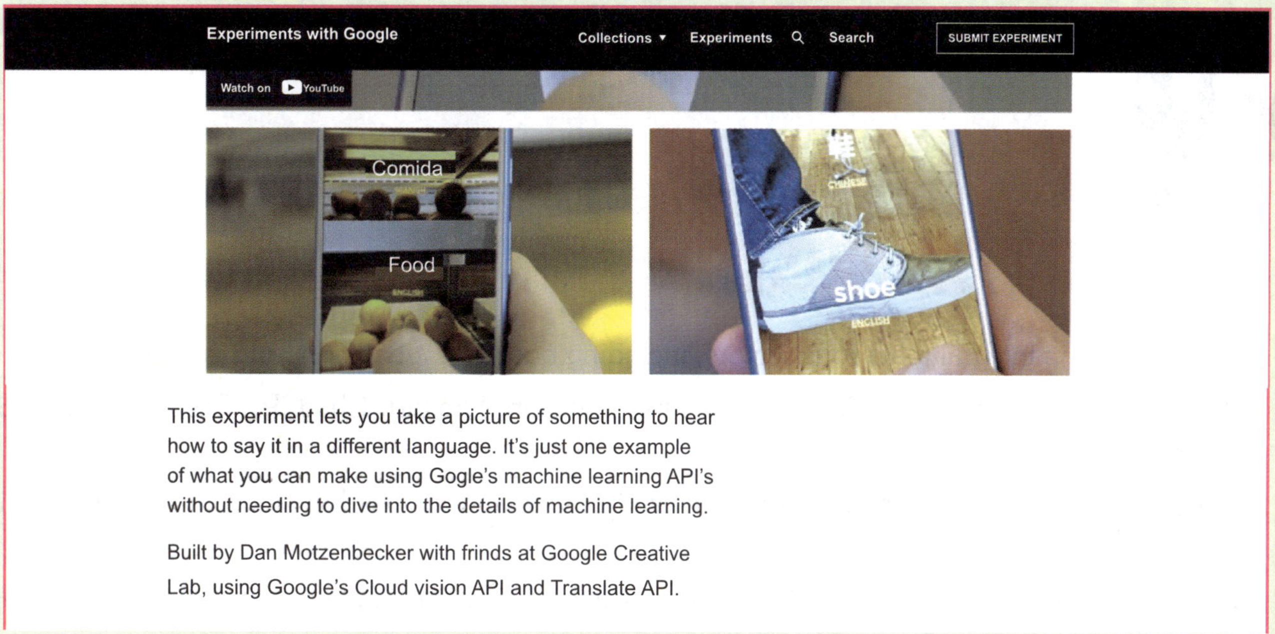

Click on Launch Experiment to start this game.

2.4 Real Life Application Names

AI applications names associated with each category:

1. **Astronomy:** Galaxy Zoo, SETI.
2. **Healthcare:** IBM Watson Health, Atomwise.
3. **Gaming:** AlphaGo, AI-driven NPCs in "The Elder Scrolls".
4. **Finance:** PayPal (Fraud Detection), Renaissance Technologies (Algorithmic Trading), Paytm, Google Pay.
5. **Data Security:** Darktrace, AEG bot.
6. **Social Media:** Facebook (Content Moderation), Twitter (now called X, Trend Analysis), Instagram, Threads.
7. **Travel & Transport:** Expedia (AI Chatbot), Google Maps, Make my Trip, ClearTrip.
8. **Automotive Industry:** Tesla Autopilot, BMW Predictive Maintenance.
9. **Robotics:** Sophia, ABB's YuMi.
10. **Entertainment:** Netflix (Content Recommendation), OpenAI's MuseNet.
11. **Agriculture:** John Deere, Blue River Technology's See & Spray.
12. **E-commerce:** Amazon (Product Recommendations), Alibaba's AliMe, Flipkart and now q(quick) commerce (examples Blinkit, Zepto, Swiggy Instamart, Big Basket.
13. **Education:** Gradescope, Carnegie Learning's AI-driven math tutor.

Scooby-Doo

Q. Write the name of the application areas where the following apps are used:

1. ______ **2.** ______

3. ______ **4.** ______

5. ______

Answer: 1. X 2. Facebook 3. Instagram 4. Snapchat

LET'S REHASH

1. AI has become integral to various sectors, including business, recreation, and education.
2. AI applications are found in daily life tools like Amazon, Flipkart, ChatGPT, Tesla Autopilot, Siri, and Google Lens etc.
3. Expert Systems in AI are designed to work like humans and are used in flight-tracking and clinical systems.
4. Natural Language Processing (NLP) allows devices to ably operate using human language, exemplified by Google Now and speech recognition.
5. Neural Networks mimic the human brain, enabling pattern recognition in areas like face and handwriting recognition.
6. Robotics involves programming machines to perform tasks, commonly seen in industrial robots used for precision tasks.
7. Fuzzy Logic Systems simulate human reasoning and are applied towards consumer electronics and automobiles.
8. AI can simulate human intelligence processes, including learning, reasoning, and self-correction.
9. John McCarthy coined the term "Artificial Intelligence" in 1956.
10. AI has applications in several industries, including healthcare, entertainment, finance, and education.
11. In astronomy, AI helps solve complex problems, such as understanding the origin of all galaxies.
12. AI in healthcare aids in medical diagnoses, patient monitoring, and drug development.
13. Gaming industries utilize AI for strategic games like chess and 3D games.
14. AI is used in finance for automation, algorithmic trading, and core fraud prevention.
15. AI enhances data security by detecting software bugs and cyber-attacks.
16. Social media platforms use AI to manage massive amounts of user data and identify trends.
17. Travel and transport sectors use AI for travel arrangements, hotel suggestions, and route planning.
18. The automotive industry leverages AI for virtual assistants and also self-driving cars.
19. AI-driven robotics can perform tasks autonomously, exemplified by humanoid robots like Sophia and Erica.
20. AI is widely used in e-commerce, agriculture, and education, in order to improve efficiency and personalize experiences.

To Solve Multiple Choice Questions Online

Scan QR Code and Check Your Score

EXERCISE

(A) Multiple Choice Questions with Answers

1. **Who coined the term "Artificial Intelligence"?**
   (a) Alan Turing (b) John McCarthy
   (c) Elon Musk (d) Isaac Asimov
2. **Which AI application is used in the automotive industry for self-driving cars?**
   (a) Sophia (b) Tesla Autopilot
   (c) IBM Watson (d) Galaxy Zoo
3. **What is the main focus of Natural Language Processing (NLP) in AI?**
   (a) Robotics (b) Human language understanding
   (c) Pattern recognition (d) Games strategy
4. **Which AI application is known for its use in content recommendation in entertainment?**
   (a) John Deere (b) Netflix
   (c) IBM Watson Health (d) PayPal
5. **Which of the following is an AI application in data security?**
   (a) AEG bot (b) AlphaGo
   (c) AliMe (d) YuMi
6. **Which sector uses AI for algorithmic trading?**
   (a) Agriculture (b) Finance
   (c) Education (d) Travel
7. **What is an example of AI in the field of astronomy?**
   (a) IBM Watson Health (b) SETI
   (c) Sophia (d) Expedia
8. **Which application is an example of AI in e-commerce?**
   (a) Ebay (b) MuseNet
   (c) See & Spray (d) DeepArt
9. **Which AI application is used in agriculture for predictive analysis?**
   (a) Blue River Technology's See & Spray (b) Tesla Autopilot
   (c) ABB's YuMi (d) Google Maps
10. **What is an AI-based application in healthcare?**
    (a) Gradescope (b) WebMD
    (c) AlphaGo (d) Facebook

11. What type of AI system is used for flight tracking?

(a) Fuzzy Logic System (b) Expert System
(c) Neural Network (d) Robotics

12. Which of the following is an example of AI in gaming?

(a) Renaissance Technologies (b) AlphaGo
(c) PayPal (d) Darktrace

13. In which industry is AI used to enhance customer service through virtual assistants?

(a) Automotive (b) Education
(c) Healthcare (d) Social Media

14. Which AI application is used in social media to manage large datasets?

(a) X (Trend Analysis) (b) Netflix
(c) Blue River Technology (d) Google Maps

15. What type of AI system is designed to work based on human reasoning?

(a) Neural Networks (b) Expert Systems
(c) Fuzzy Logic Systems (d) Robotics

16. Which AI application is an example of an educational tool?

(a) Gradescope (b) Tesla Autopilot
(c) Darktrace (d) IBM Watson Health

17. What is an example of AI-driven personal assistant in travel and transport?

(a) Google Maps (b) AliMe
(c) Galaxy Zoo (d) Atomwise

18. Which AI technology is used for handwriting recognition?

(a) Neural Networks (b) Robotics
(c) Fuzzy Logic Systems (d) Expert Systems

19. In which field is AI used to predict consumption patterns?

(a) Finance (b) Agriculture
(c) Social Media (d) E-commerce

20. Which AI application is used in the field of entertainment?

(a) MuseNet (b) John Deere
(c) AliMe (d) ABB's YuMi

ANSWERS

1.	(b)	2.	(b)	3.	(b)	4.	(b)	5.	(a)
6.	(b)	7.	(b)	8.	(a)	9.	(a)	10.	(b)
11.	(b)	12.	(b)	13.	(a)	14.	(a)	15.	(c)
16.	(a)	17.	(a)	18.	(a)	19.	(d)	20.	(a)

(B) Fill in the Blanks with Answers

1. AI applications are commonly found in __________ like Amazon, Flipkart, Swiggy and Tesla Autopilot.

Ans. daily life

2. The term "Artificial Intelligence" was coined by __________ in 1956.

Ans. John McCarthy

3. AI in __________ helps solve many of the complex universe problems.

Ans. astronomy

4. __________ is an AI mostly application used for content recommendation in entertainment.

Ans. Netflix

5. __________ is a technology used in finance for algorithmic trading.

Ans. Renaissance Technologies

6. Neural networks in AI mimic the functioning of __________ in the human body.

Ans. neurons

7. The __________ industry uses AI for virtual assistants like TeslaBot.

Ans. automotive

8. __________ is an exact example of AI in robotics that can talk and behave like humans.

Ans. Sophia

9. __________ is an AI application used for fraud detection in finance.

Ans. PayPal

10. AI-driven tools like __________ are used for grading in education.

Ans. Gradescope

11. AI can be applied in agriculture through __________ for crop monitoring and predictive analysis.

Ans. Blue River Technology's See & Spray

12. __________ is an example of an AI-driven virtual tutor in education.

Ans. Carnegie Learning's AI-driven math tutor

13. AI in __________ is generally used to manage user data and identify trends.

Ans. social media

14. __________ is a common AI application used in travel to suggest routes and accommodations.

Ans. Google Maps

15. AI applications in the field of healthcare include __________ for drug development.

Ans. Atomwise

(C) Short Questions with Answers

1. **What is the role of AI in day to dayhealthcare?**

Ans. AI in healthcare assists with medical diagnoses, patient monitoring, and drug development.

2. **Which AI application is used for content moderation in social media?**

Ans. Facebook uses AI for content moderation in social media.

3. **How is AI applied in the gaming industry?**

Ans. AI is used in gaming to design and play strategic games like chess and to create AI-driven non-playable characters (NPCs).

4. What is an example of AI in data security?

Ans. Darktrace is an apt example of AI used in data security.

5. How does AI contribute towards e-commerce?

Ans. AI in e-commerce helps with product recommendations, demand forecasting, and fraud detection.

6. Which AI application is used in agriculture for predictive analysis?

Ans. Blue River Technology's See & Spray is used in agriculture for a lot of predictive analysis.

7. What is the purpose of using AI in finance?

Ans. AI in finance is used for automation, algorithmic trading, and fraud prevention.

8. Which AI application is an example in the automotive industry?

Ans. Tesla Autopilot is a right example of AI in the automotive industry.

9. How is AI applied in education?

Ans. AI is used in education towards automated grading, virtual tutoring, and personalized learning.

10. Which AI tool is used in travel for route planning?

Ans. Google Maps is commonly used in travel for route planning.

ACTIVITY-BASED QUESTIONS

1. Research and present a real-world example of AI being used in agriculture. Explain how it mostly improves farming practices.
2. Create a chart to show the various applications that are associated with AI.

TEACHER'S NOTES

2.1 Introduction

- AI is used in business, education, entertainment, transport, and daily life.

Activity: Students name apps or devices using AI (Google, YouTube, Alexa).

2.2 Research Areas

- Main areas: Expert Systems, NLP, Neural Networks, Robotics, Fuzzy Logic.

Activity: Show 5 pictures—students match each to the research area.

2.3 Application of AI

- AI helps in Astronomy, Healthcare, Gaming, Finance, Security, Travel, etc.

Activity: Students make mini posters showing AI use i n one sector.

2.4 Real-Life Application Names

- Examples: Tesla Autopilot, Netflix, PayPal, IBM Watson, Google Maps, Sophia.

Activity: Play "AI Match-up" – teacher names an app, students guess its field.

CHAPTER 3

DOMAINS OF AI

Domains of AI
in Action

Scan QR Code

OBJECTIVES

TOPICS TO BE COVERED

- Introduction to domain
- Types of domain
- Introduction to AI Domains using applications (Data, CV & NLP)

3.1 Introduction to Domain

Artificial Intelligence is a revolutionary technology that has changed the thinking process of the entire world. AI is the creation of machines that can mimic human capabilities such as learning, reasoning, and problem-solving. From self-driving cars to personalized virtual assistants, AI's is leaving its noticable impact by transforming the way we work, live, and interact with technology.

AI work in many areas but it is important to understand the type of work an AI machine can do in a given specific area. Based on application area, we categorize AI in three domains:

1. Data Science,
2. Computer Vision,
3. NLP(Natural Language Processing).

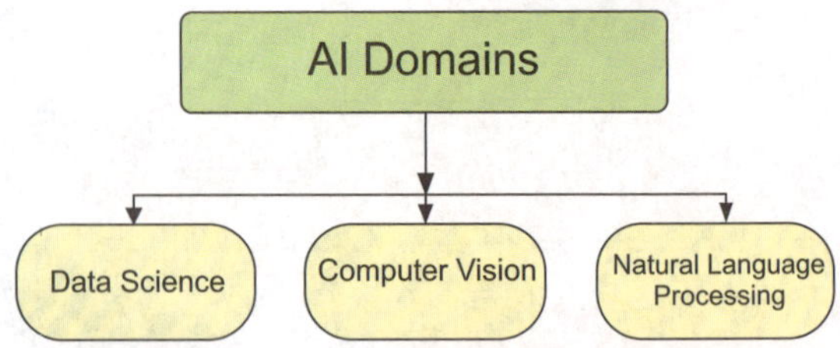

3.2 Types of Domain

The **domains in AI** include various specialized areas wherein intelligent machines and algorithms are developed to meet the specific challenges and applications. These domains include:

Treasure Link
Domains of AI in Action
Scan QR Code

1. **Data Sciences:** It is a multidisciplinary field that combines mathematics, statistics, and computer science to apply machine learning algorithms to obtain numbers, text, images, video, audio etc. to produce artificial intelligence (AI) systems that perform tasks like a human does. The data whether numeric, text, audio, video, image, etc. is all converted to numeric form for extraction, preparation, analysis, visualization, and maintenance of information.

2. **Computer Vision:** Computer Vision (CV) is the scientific technology for building artificial systems that obtain information from images, video or any other visual data. This involves mostly the methods of acquiring, processing, analyzing, and understanding digital images, and extraction of data from the real and visual world to produce information.

3. **Natural Language Processing:** Natural Language Processing (NLP), is a branch of artificial intelligence that deals with the interaction between computers and humans using the natural language such as English, spanish, Hindi etc. In this domain, AI allows machines to fully understand, interpret, and generate human language. It works with text and speech based data.

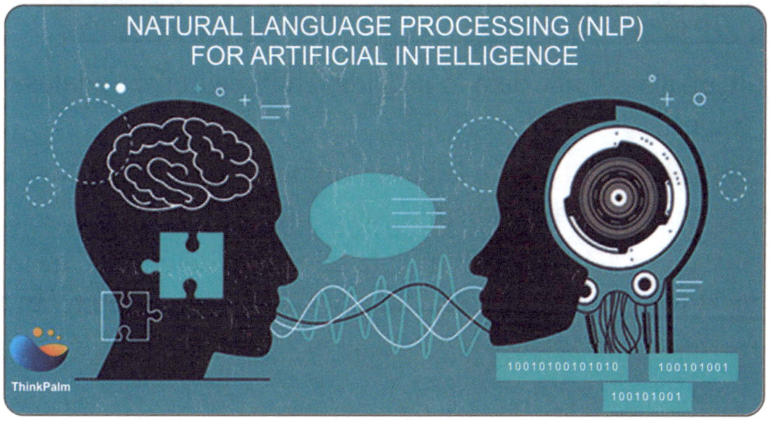

3.3 Introduction to AI Domains Using Applications (Data, CV & NLP)

All the three domains cover all the areas of Artificial Intelligence. These domains cover specific fields. Now a days, domain have become specific in generative AI . Domain-specific generative AI is a special approach for creating data by rightly training models on specific data sets related to particular domains. For example, we can create image using text through Generative-AI tools like Adobe Firefly, Zapier, Canva, etc.

Treasure Link
What is Generative AI? in Action
Scan QR Code

3.3.1 Application of Data Science

1. **Price Comparison Websites:** The websites that are being driven by lots and lots of data are usually meant for comparison purposes. They gather data and then also analyse it. Customer look for such websites that provide the convenience of comparing the price of a product from multiple vendors at one place. PriceGrabber, PriceRunner, Junglee, Shopzilla, DealTime are some examples of price comparison websites.

Scooby-Doo Quest

Q. Name any two Tools that are related to Generative AI.

1. ______________
2. ______________

Answers: 1. Zapier 2. Adobe Firefly

2. **News Feed Personalization on Facebook:** The news feed personalization help each user by analyzing their interactions, likes, dislikes, comment, etc. It also uses machine learning to detect and filter inappropriate content, ensuring community standards are thereby maintained.

Treasure Link
Understand Data Science in Action
Scan QR Code

3. **Google Maps:** It analyzes traffic data to provide real-time traffic updates and optimal driving routes.
4. **Personalized Search by Zillow:** It is based on based on user preferences and browsing history for property search results.
5. **Route Optimization by Uber:** It utilizes data science to determine the most efficient routes for drivers, reducing travel time and fuel consumption., in the process.

Treasure Link
Application of Data Science in Action
Scan QR Code

FUN.AI ACTIVITY

Visit the site: https://www.codingame.com/ide/puzzle/onboarding

Treasure Link
Coding Games in Action
Scan QR Code

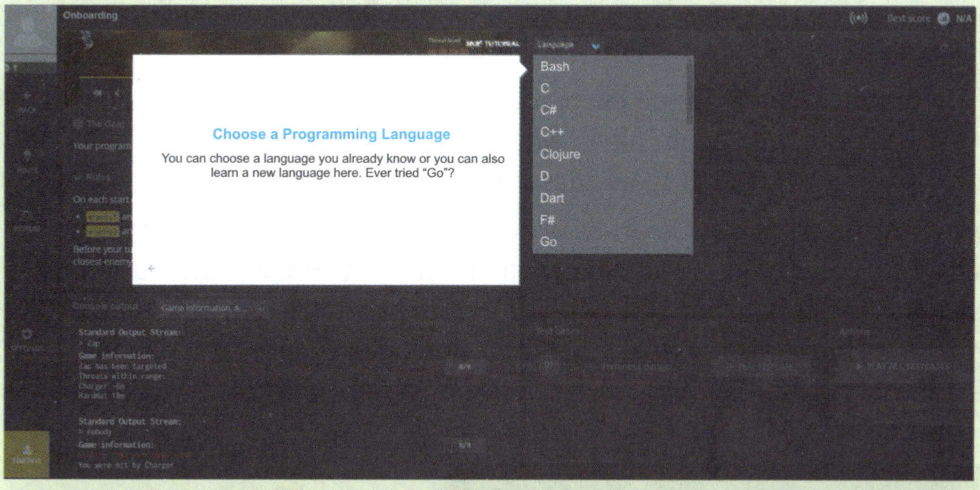

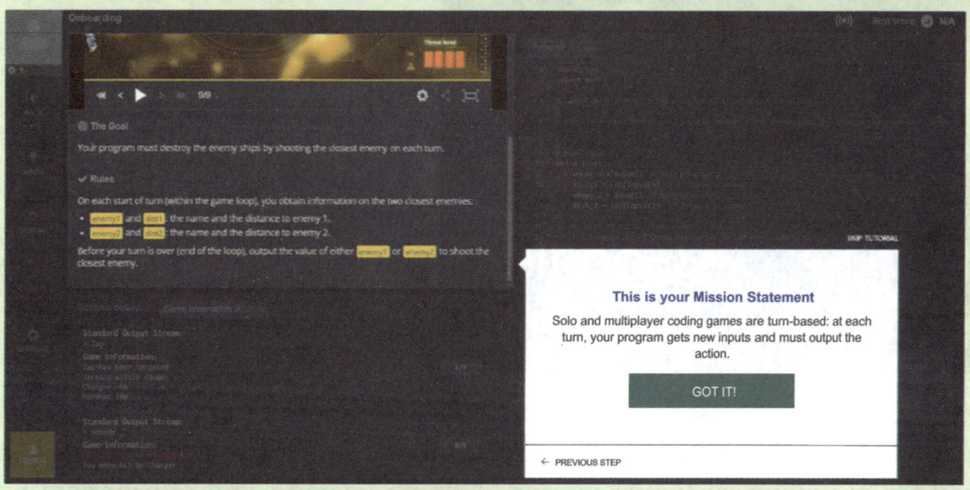

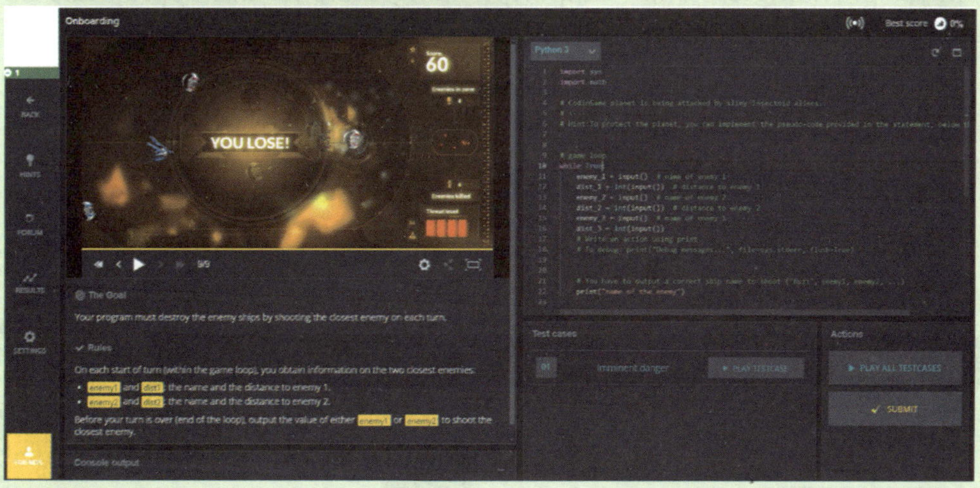

3.3.2 Applications of NLP

1. **Speech Recognition on Mobile Phone:** NLP controls speech recognition systems by converting the concerned spoken language into text. This technology is used in voice-controlled devices, voice assistants, and dictation software.
2. **Language Translation on Google Translate:** NLP facilitates language translation, enabling machines to translate text from one language to another.

Treasure Link
Natural Language Processing in Action

Scan QR Code

Translation services, language learning apps, and global communication are benefitted from this type of application.

3. **Email Filters on Gmail:** Email filters are one of the most basic and initial applications of NLP online. It started out with spam filters where we can easily mention certain words or phrases that signal a spam message.

Treasure Link
Application of NLP in Action
Scan QR Code

4. **Smart/virtual Assistants:** Smart assistants like Apple's Siri and Amazon's Alexa recognize patterns in speech, then gather meaning and provide a useful response. NLP is the backbone of popular virtual assistants like Siri, Alexa, and Google Assistant. These assistants then understand spoken language, process user queries, and provide relevant responses or perform tasks based on the context.

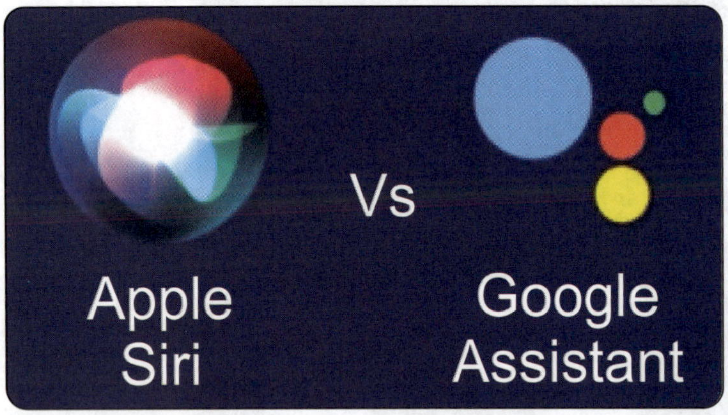

Scooby-Doo Quest

Q. Name any two Virtual assistants that you use in your daily life.

1. ____________
2. ____________

Ans. 1. Apple's Siri 2. Amazon's Alexa

5. **Chatbots:** Chatbots are used with many application these days. NLP is essential for chatbots, enabling them to engage in human-like conversations with the relevant users. These chatbots are employed for providing customer support, helping users to find appropriate information, and providing personalized recommendations.

FUN.AI ACTIVITY

Visit the site: https://experiments.withgoogle.com/semantris

1. Click on Launch experiment.

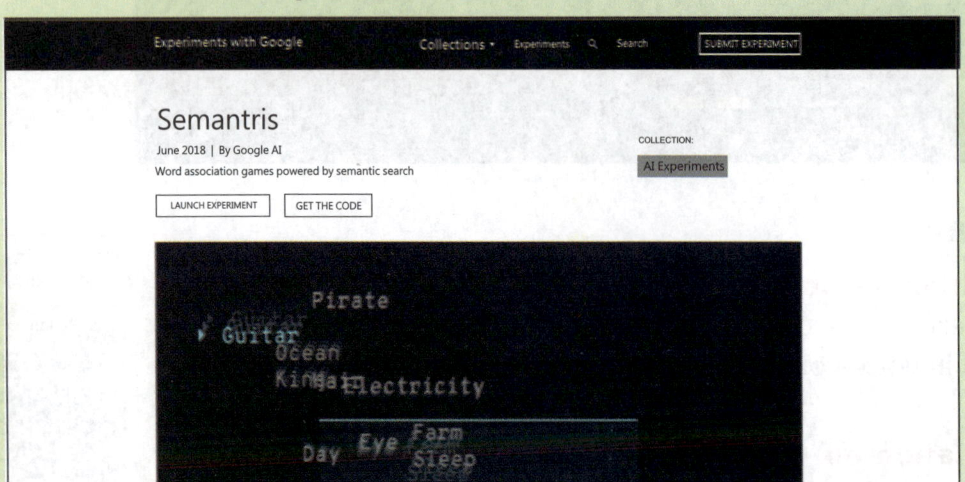

Treasure Link
Launch Experiment in Action
Scan QR Code

2. The following screen appears.

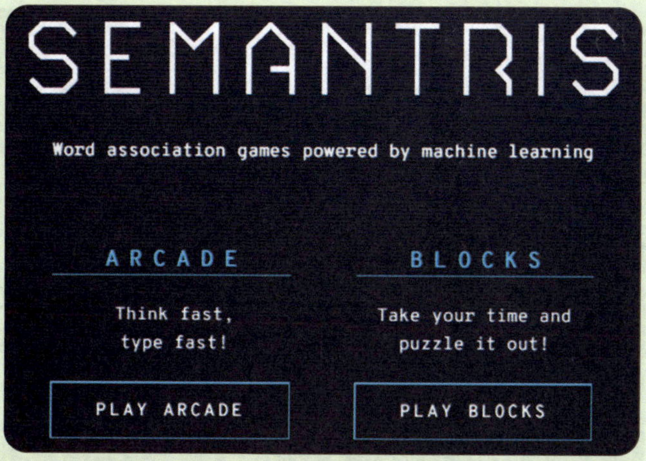

3. Click on play arcade.

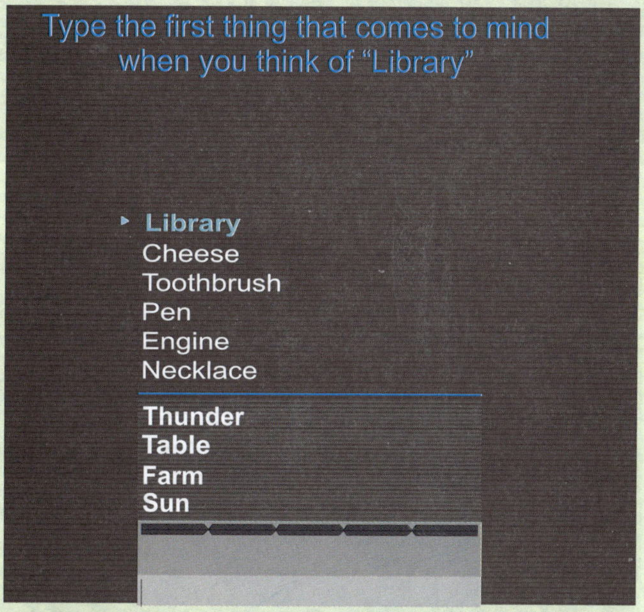

4. Write the most nearest word.

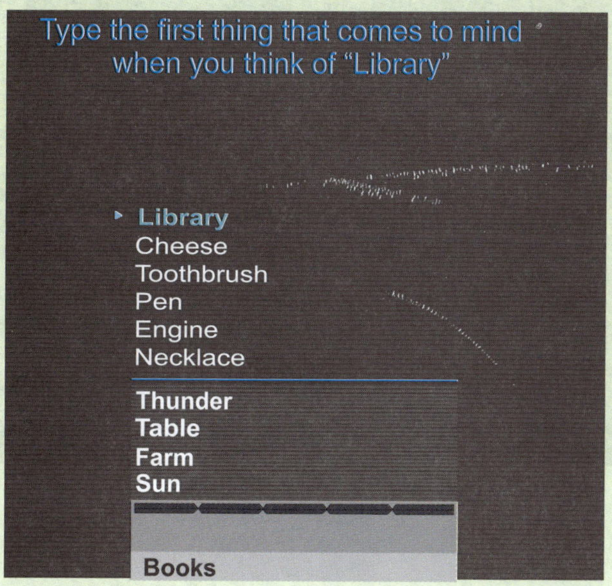

5. If the word is correct , you will earn required points.

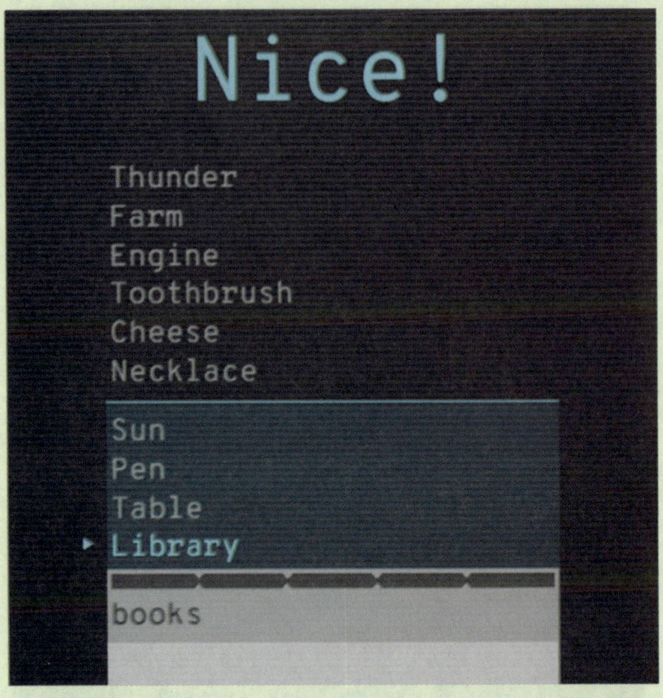

Keep guessing !!!

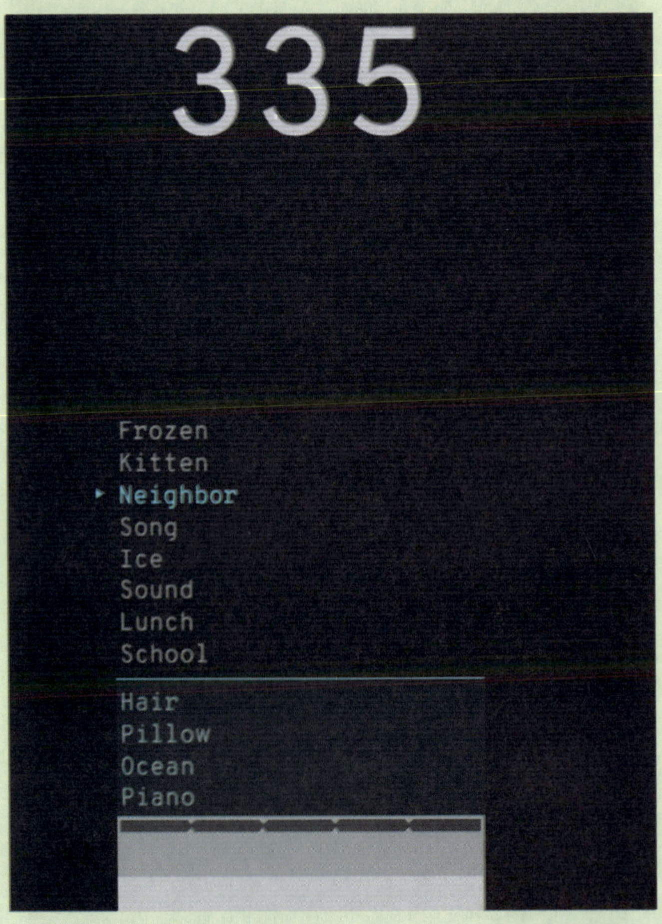

3.3.3 Application of Computer Vision

1. **Autonomous Vehicles by Tesla:** CV systems scan live objects and easily analyse them, based on whether the car decides to keep running or to stop. Computer vision plays an important role in enabling self-driving cars to navigate, detect obstacles, and interpret traffic signs and signals. Identifying road lanes and maintaining the vehicle's position within them by using computer vision algorithms is an important feature of autonomous vehicles.

Treasure Link
Computer Vision in Action
Scan QR Code

Treasure Link
Application of Computer Vision in Action
Scan QR Code

2. **Pedestrian Detection by Tesla:** Detecting pedestrians and other hurdles on the road enhances safety for users in all the autonomous driving systems.
3. **Surveillance Systems:** Computer vision is extensively used in surveillance for security and monitoring purposes.
4. **Video Analytics:** Computer vision help in analysing real-time video feeds to detect suspicious activities, unauthorized access, or any unusual behaviour.
5. **Face Lock in Smartphones:** Today, smartphones come with the feature of face locks in which the smartphone's owner can set up his/her face as an unlocking mechanism for it. The front camera rightly detects and captures the face and saves its features during beginning. Next time onwards, whenever the features match, the phone is unlocked. This helps the user by not allowing any stranger to open the mobile.

Scooby-Doo Quest

Q. Does your father use face lock on his smart phone? Is it safe to lock your phone using face lock? Ask your father and write the process of setting face lock.

____

____

Answers: Yes, my father use face lock on phone and it is safe.
Open Settings in smart phone and then use lock screen option and then choose face lock feature

FUN.AI ACTIVITY

Treasure Link
Freepik AI
in Action

Scan QR Code

Visit The site: https://www.freepik.com/free-photos-vectors/arena-ai

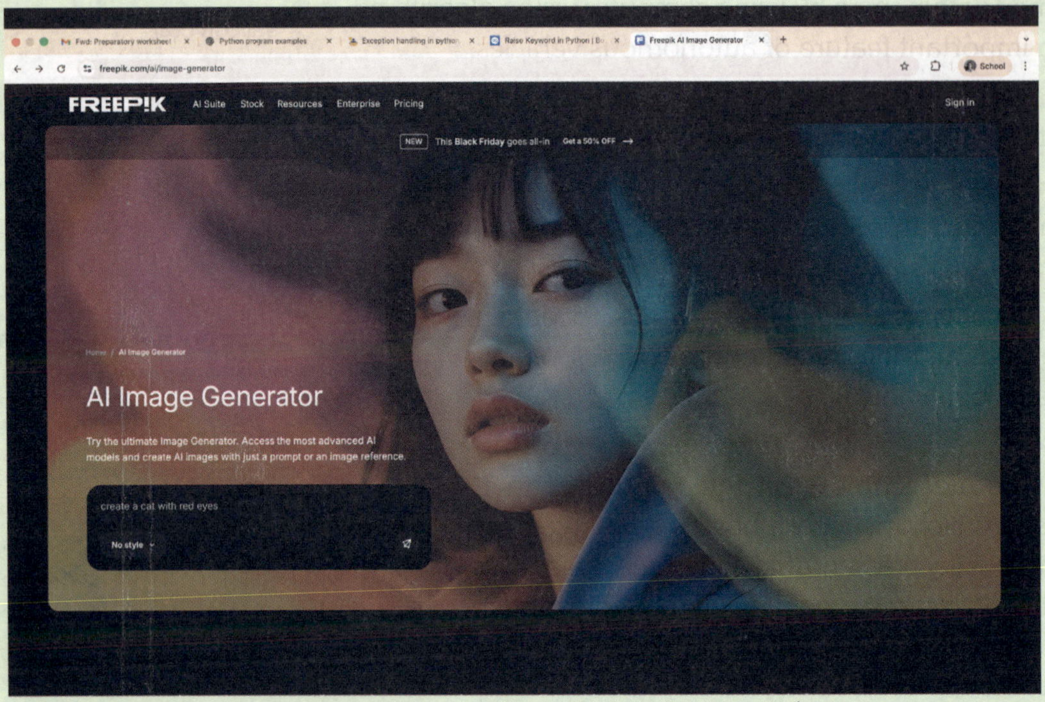

Enter the prompt for the image you want to generate and click on generate

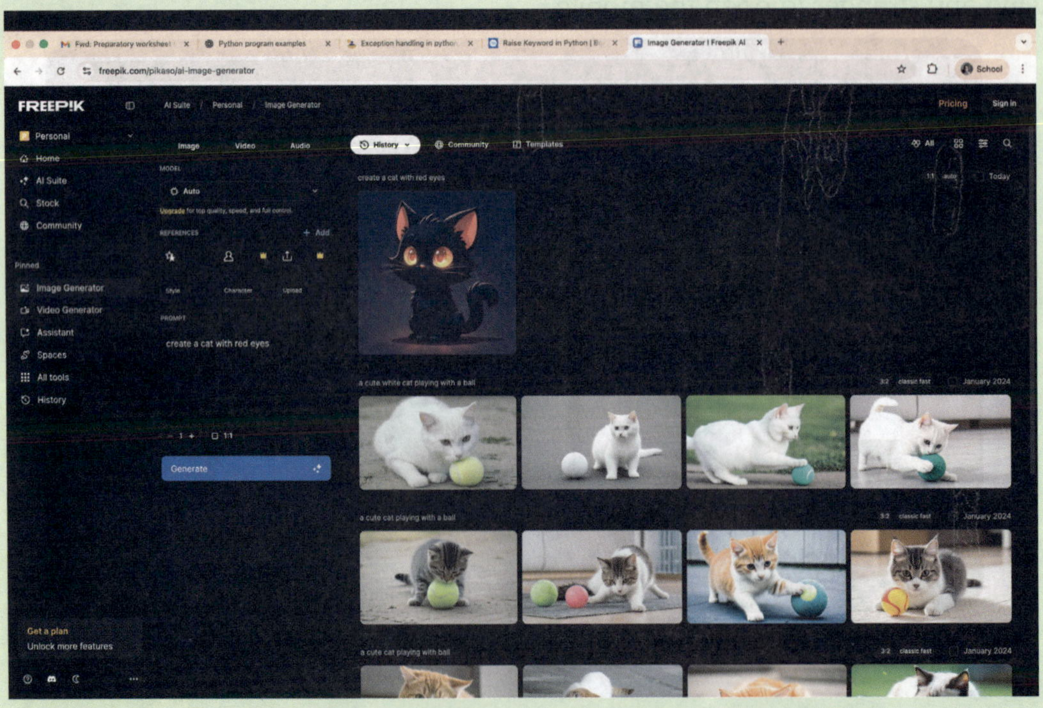

Keep Finding !!!

LET'S REHASH

1. **Artificial Intelligence (AI)** involves the creation of machines that can mimic human capabilities such as learning, reasoning, and the right kind of problem-solving.
2. AI has transformed how we work, live, and interact with technology, with applications vastly ranging from self-driving cars to personalized virtual assistants.
3. AI is divided into three main domains based on application areas: **Data Science, Computer Vision, and Natural Language Processing (NLP).**
4. **Data Science** is a multidisciplinary field that fully applies machine learning algorithms to various forms of data, such as numbers, text, images, video, and audio, to create AI systems.
5. In Data Science, all forms of data are converted into numeric form for extraction, analysis, and also visualization.
6. **Computer Vision (CV)** is a scientific technology that builds systems capable of obtaining and processing information from images and various visual data.
7. Computer Vision involves acquiring, processing, and analyzing digital images to extract useful information from the existing real world.
8. **Natural Language Processing (NLP)** is a branch of AI focused on the interaction between computers and humans using natural language, like text and speech.
9. NLP enables machines to understand, interpret, and generate human language, facilitating applications such as speech recognition, language translation, and also from chatbots.
10. The three AI domains cover all aspects of artificial intelligence, and domain-specific generative AI focuses on training models specifically using data specific to particular domains.
11. **Data Science Applications** include price comparison websites, news feed personalization on social media, Google Maps for all real-time traffic updates, personalized property search results, and Uber's route optimization.
12. **Price Comparison Websites** use large datasets to allow users to compare the prices of products from different vendors at one given location.
13. **Facebook's News Feed Personalization** utilizes user interactions and machine learning to tailor content and filter any inappropriate posts.
14. **Google Maps** applies Data Science to analyze traffic data and provide optimal driving routes in real time.
15. **NLP Applications** include speech recognition, language translation, email filters, virtual assistants, and chatbots, which help machines that engage in human-like conversations.
16. **Speech Recognition** converts spoken language into text and is then used in devices like smartphones and virtual assistants.
17. **Computer Vision Applications** include autonomous vehicles, pedestrian detection, surveillance systems, video analytics, and manyface recognition, towards smartphone locks.

18. **Autonomous Vehicles** like those by Tesla rely on Computer Vision to detect obstacles, identify road signs, and thereby ensure safe navigation.
19. **Face Lock** technology in smartphones uses Computer Vision to scan and recognize a particular user's face for secure unlocking.
20. **Generative AI** is a specialized approach that creates new data by training models on specific datasets, such as generating images from the text using tools like Adobe Firefly or Canva.

To Solve Multiple Choice Questions Online

Scan QR Code and Check Your Score

EXERCISE

(A) Multiple Choice Questions with Answers

1. **What is Artificial Intelligence (AI)?**
   (a) The ability to create complex programs
   (b) Machines that mimic/copy human capabilities
   (c) The process of converting data into information
   (d) A new programming language
2. **Which of the following is a domain of AI?**
   (a) Mechanical Engineering (b) Data Science
   (c) Electrical Engineering (d) Biology
3. **Which AI domain deals with images and video data?**
   (a) Natural Language Processing (NLP) (b) Data Science
   (c) Computer Vision (d) Cloud Computing
4. **What does NLP stand for?**
   (a) Neural Learning Processing (b) Natural Language Programming
   (c) Natural Language Processing (d) Network Language Protocol
5. **Which of the following is an application of Data Science?**
   (a) Face Lock in Smartphones (b) Google Maps
   (c) Speech Recognition (d) Chatbots
6. **Which of the following is a classic example of a Price Comparison website?**
   (a) Siri (b) Shopzilla
   (c) Facebook (d) Google Translate
7. **What is an exact example of a Natural Language Processing application?**
   (a) Autonomous vehicles (b) Pedestrian detection
   (c) Language translation (d) Surveillance systems

8. Which application uses data to provide all the real-time traffic updates?

(a) Google Maps (b) Uber

(c) Gmail (d) Tesla

9. Which AI domain helps in analyzing any real-time video feeds?

(a) Data Science (b) Computer Vision

(c) NLP (d) None of the above

10. Which company uses Computer Vision towards autonomous vehicles?

(a) Google (b) Apple

(c) Tesla (d) Amazon

11. Which technology is the backbone of virtual assistants such as Siri and Alexa?

(a) Data Science (b) Computer Vision

(c) NLP (d) Surveillance Systems

12. Which AI domain is involved in creating the artificial systems from visual data?

(a) NLP (b) Computer Vision

(c) Machine Learning (d) Neural Networks

13. What is an application of NLP on Gmail?

(a) Route optimization (b) Email filters

(c) Keeping Surveillance (d) Face lock

14. Which AI domain is used to create data from specific datasets in the Generative AI?

(a) Data Science (b) Computer Vision

(c) NLP (d) All of the above

15. What is the goal of a Natural Language Processing?

(a) Generate images

(b) Understand and generate human language

(c) Analyze video feeds

(d) Optimize routes for all drivers

16. What is a common application of Computer Vision in smartphones?

(a) Chatbots (b) Face lock

(c) Route optimization (d) Price comparison

17. Which AI domain involves the extraction of information from all the real-world visual data?

(a) NLP (b) Data Science

(c) Computer Vision (d) None of the above

18. Which AI domain enables machines to translate text from one language to another?

(a) NLP (b) Data Science

(c) Computer Vision (d) Machine Learning

19. Which application generally helps optimize routes for Uber drivers?

(a) Speech recognition (b) Google Maps
(c) Route optimization (d) Personalized search

20. Which of these is an example of the speech recognition?

(a) Tesla (b) Google Translate
(c) Siri (d) Uber

ANSWERS

1.	(b)	2.	(b)	3.	(c)	4.	(c)	5.	(b)
6.	(b)	7.	(c)	8.	(a)	9.	(b)	10.	(c)
11.	(c)	12.	(b)	13.	(b)	14.	(d)	15.	(b)
16.	(b)	17.	(c)	18.	(a)	19.	(c)	20.	(c)

(B) Fill in the Blanks with Answers

1. AI is the creation or a byproduct of machines , that can mimic human capabilities such as __________, reasoning, and problem-solving.

Ans. learning

2. The three main domains of AI are Data Science, Computer Vision, and __________.

Ans. Natural Language Processing (NLP)

3. __________ is a branch of AI that deals with interpreting and generating human language.

Ans. NLP

4. Computer Vision is primarily concerned with extracting information from __________.

Ans. images and video

5. __________ websites allow users to compare prices of products across different vendors.

Ans. Price Comparison

6. One example of AI in all autonomous vehicles is __________, which uses Computer Vision.

Ans. Tesla

7. Machine learning algorithms are used in __________ to analyze large datasets.

Ans. Data Science

8. NLP is essential for smart virtual assistants like __________ and Alexa.

Ans. Siri

9. Google Maps uses data to provide real-time __________ updates.

Ans. traffic

10. __________ are basic applications of an NLP for sorting and managing emails.

Ans. Email filters

11. __________ helps to detect pedestrians in autonomous driving systems.

Ans. Computer Vision

12. __________ AI uses specific datasets to create new data.

Ans. Generative

13. Face lock in smartphones is an example of __________ application.

Ans. Computer Vision

14. __________ helps Uber cab drivers reduce travel time by finding efficient routes.

Ans. Route optimization

15. __________ in NLP allows machines to translate from one language to another.

Ans. Language translation

(C) Short Questions with Answers

1. What is Artificial Intelligence (AI)?

Ans. AI is the creation of machines that can mimic human abilities such as learning, reasoning, and to a large extent, problem-solving.

2. Name the three domains of AI.

Ans. Data Science, Computer Vision, and Natural Language Processing (NLP).

3. What is the role of Data Science in AI?

Ans. Data Science involves applying machine learning algorithms to data for tasks like analysis, visualization, and information extraction.

4. What is Computer Vision?

Ans. Computer Vision is a technology that allows machines to obtain and process visual data from images and videos.

5. What is the purpose of the Natural Language Processing?

Ans. NLP allows machines to understand, interpret, and generate human language in a way that is useful for various applications.

6. Give one example of an application of Data Science.

Ans. Google Maps, which uses data to provide real-time traffic updates.

7. What is Generative AI?

Ans. Generative AI is a method for creating new data by training models on specific datasets related to particular domains.

8. How does NLP benefit virtual assistants?

Ans. NLP allows virtual assistants like Siri and Alexa to fully understand and respond to spoken commands from users.

9. What role does Computer Vision play in autonomous vehicles?

Ans. Computer Vision helps vehicles detect obstacles, recognize road signs, and interpret traffic signals for safe driving.

10. What is speech recognition in the context of NLP?

Ans. Speech recognition involves converting spoken language into given text for processing in applications like virtual assistants and voice-controlled devices.

ACTIVITY-BASED QUESTIONS

1. **Activity:** Create a drawing using generative AI tools like Adobe Firefly or Canva on "Social media".
2. **Activity:** Choose one application of NLP (such as a chatbot or virtual assistant) and create a presentation explaining how it works and what technologies are used.

TEACHER'S NOTES

3.1 Introduction to Domains

- Three main domains: Data Science, Computer Vision, NLP.

Activity: Show logos (Google Maps, Alexa, Face Lock) – students classify under correct domain.

3.2 Data Science

- Works with data (numbers, text) for analysis and predictions.

Activity: Show Google Maps – ask how it predicts traffic using data.

3.3 Computer Vision

- Helps machines understand visual data (images/videos).

Activity: Use Google Lens or camera to identify nearby objects.

3.4 Natural Language Processing (NLP)

- Enables computers to understand human language (text/speech).

Activity: Use voice typing or Google Translate to demonstrate NLP.

3.5 Generative AI

- Creates new data (images/text) using trained models.

Activity: Students use Canva or Firefly to create an AI-generated image.

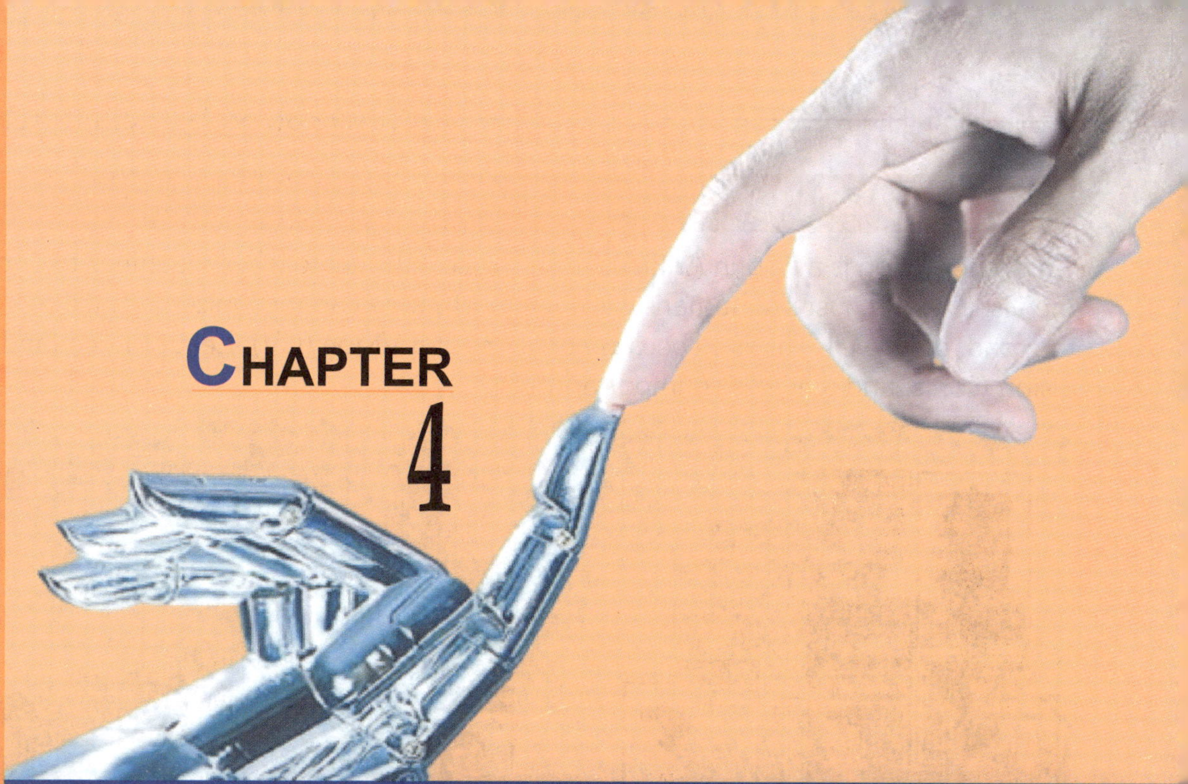

CHAPTER

4

COMPUTER VISION (CV) IN AI

Computer Vision (CV) in AI
in Action

Scan QR Code

OBJECTIVES

TOPICS TO BE COVERED

- Introduction
- Computer Vision
- How Computer Vision Works in AI
- Examples of Computer Vision in Action
- Importance of Computer Vision
- Computer Vision Games

4.1 Introduction

Computer vision is a field in Artificial Intelligence (AI) that teaches machines to understand and interpret the visual world, just like humans do. Our smartphone can recognize our face. A self-driving car can see the road, quite well. This is all because of Computer Vision (CV). Let us understand about how computer vision works, and why it is so important.

4.2 Computer Vision

Computer Vision is when we provide eyes to machines. The machine captures the image in front of it. It helps computers to "see" and understand images and videos. In this process, there are two things:

1. **Capture:** When you look at a picture, your eyes send information to your brain. Your brain captures the various co-ordinates of the image.
2. **Understanding:** Once the image is captured, our brain processes this information and tells us the actual thing the image resembles what it see (e.g., "That's a Dog!").
3. **Identification:** The images of different objects and living beings are already saved inside the machine so the machine tries to match it with the image captured. Once the image is matched, it tells the name of the thing.

Treasure Link
How Computer Vision Works in Action
Scan QR Code

In Computer Vision, we use cameras and sensors to capture images, and then we use algorithms (a set of rules or instructions) to help the computer understand what's in those images.

4.3 How Computer Vision Works in AI

Imagine you are a superman who can see and understand everything around him instantly. Computer Vision is more like giving that power of a superman to computers. It helps them see and understand images and videos just like we do. Let us understand the steps in detail:

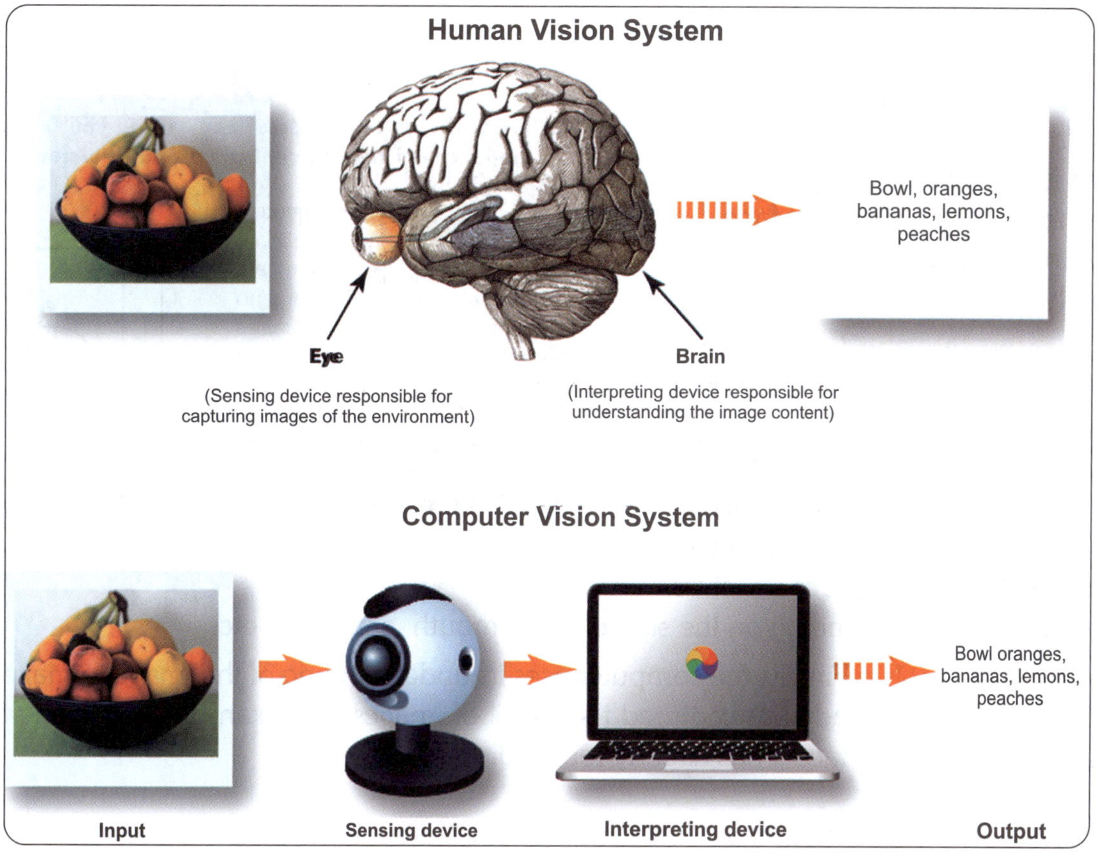

1. **Detecting image with Cameras and Sensors:** First, the computer detect the image of the in front of it. It uses cameras and sensors to capture images and videos. These devices take pictures of what's around them.For example, a camera on your phone takes your selfie.
2. **Processing the Images:** Once the computer has the images, it needs to process them to understand what is there in the image. In this step our brain tries to find out what it see in the image. To do so, the computer looks towards the hidden patterns in the image like edges, shapes, and colors. For example, it can find the edges of a car or the shape of a tree or the shape of the face by using coordinates.

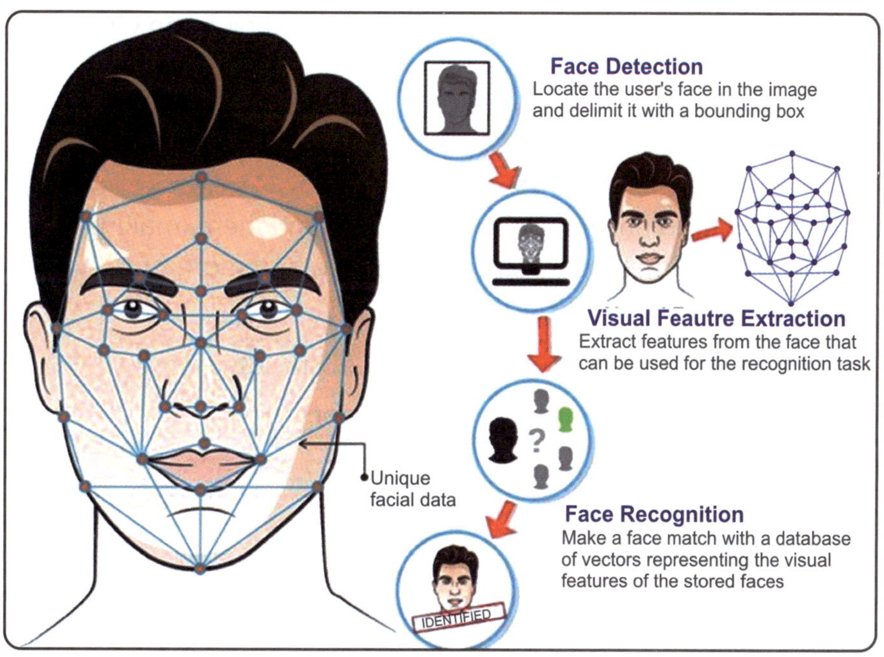

3. **Extracting Features:** Next, the computer identifies important parts of the image, called features. These details help the computer understand what is in depicted the picture. For example, recognizing a face by looking at the eyes, nose, and mouth.

4. **Understanding the Image:** Now, the computer uses what it has learned to understand the image. It uses algorithms (a set of rules or instructions) to make sense of the features it found. For example, deciding that the image is a picture of a cat or a dog depending on the shape of the mouth, ear, body, etc.

5. **Making Decisions:** Finally, the computer uses its understanding of the image to make decisions or take actions. It already has captured the detail of images. For example, Unlocking the phone after it recognizes the face it has already recoded.

Scooby-Doo Quest

Q. Draw the co-ordinates of any fruit in your copy and explain the concept of computer vision.

Ans. Computer vision is a way that computers "see" and understand pictures and videos, similar to how we use eyes. Imagine taking hoto of an apple. The computer breaks it down into tiny dots and patterns, then uses math to figure out the shape, color, and parts of the apple. This way, it can recognize objects like fruits, animals, and people!

4.4 Examples of Computer Vision in Action

1. **Face Recognition:** The computer sees your face, finds the features (eyes, nose, mouth), and then recognizes you. Example: Unlocking phones, tagging friends in photos on social media.
2. **Object Detection:** The computer sees objects in an image and identifies them. Example: Self-driving cars recognizing other cars, people, and obstacles.
3. **Image Search:** When we upload a picture, and the computer finds similar images. Example: Google Image Search.
4. **Augmented Reality (AR):** The computer sees the real world through your camera and also in the process, adds digital images on top. Example: Games like Pokémon GO, where digital characters appear in the real world.

4.5 Importance of Computer Vision

Computer Vision helps machines to understand the world around them, making them smarter and more helpful. It's used in many areas to make our lives easier, safer, and more fun.

- **Smartphones:** Face recognition for security.
- **Self-Driving Cars:** Seeing the road and avoiding obstacles.
- **Healthcare:** Analyzing medical images to help doctors.
- **Entertainment:** Creating many immersive games and experiences.

Treasure Link
How can a self-driving car works?
in Action
Scan QR Code

Computer vision is important because:

1. **It enhances everyday Life by making things easier:**
    - **Smartphones:** Face recognition makes unlocking phones faster and more secure.
    - **Social Media:** Automatic tagging of friends in photos makes sharing easier.
2. **It improves safety:**
    - **Self-Driving Cars:** Detecting obstacles and other vehicles to substantially prevent accidents.
    - **Security Systems:** Monitoring surveillance cameras to identify suspicious activities.
3. **It promotes healthcare:**
    - **Medical Imaging:** Helping doctors to analyze X-rays and MRIs for better diagnosis.
    - **Surgery Assistance:** Guiding robots to perform precise surgeries.
4. **It boost Industrial Efficiency:**
    - **Quality Control:** Inspecting products on an assembly line, for defects.
    - **Robotics:** Helping robots to navigate and interact with objects in factories.
5. **It supports Education in schools:**
    - **Interactive Learning:** Using augmented reality to make learning more engaging.
    - **Reading Assistance:** Helping visually impaired students to read and understand texts.

Scooby-Doo Quest

Q. How can we use Computer vision in the following areas?

1. Smart phone: ____________
2. Health care: ____________
3. Entertainment ____________

Answers: 1. Face recognition 2. Surgery Assistance 3. Immersive games

4.6 Computer Vision Games

Game 1 in Action

Scan QR Code

Games that are related to computer vision are:

Game 1: https://www.eyegazegames.com/game?id=mole_miners

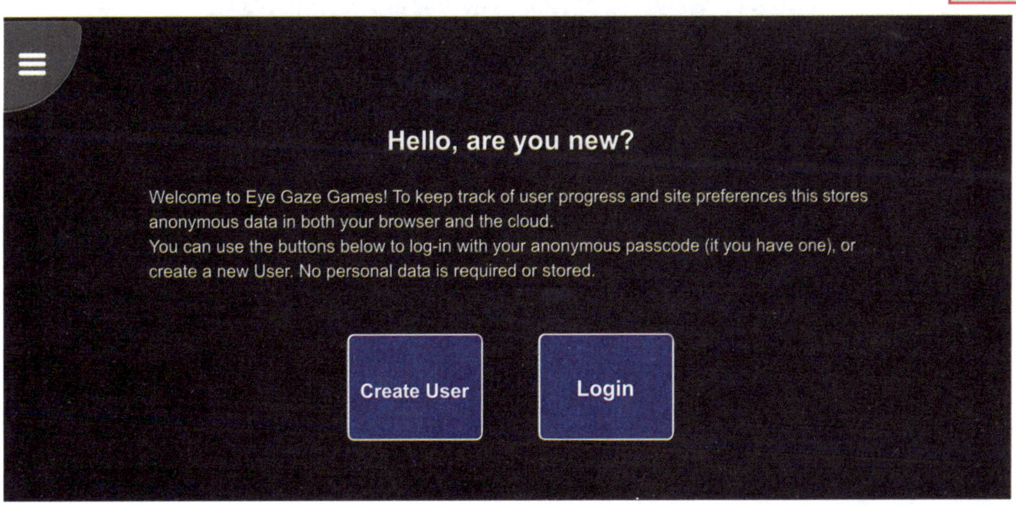

MOLE MINERS
How to Play
Start

GEMSTONE CAVERNS
Greetings intrepid explorer!
I'm Chip, and I'm going to show you how to get started!

Wow! Look at that shiny gem.
Let's fire a cannonball at it and mine it!

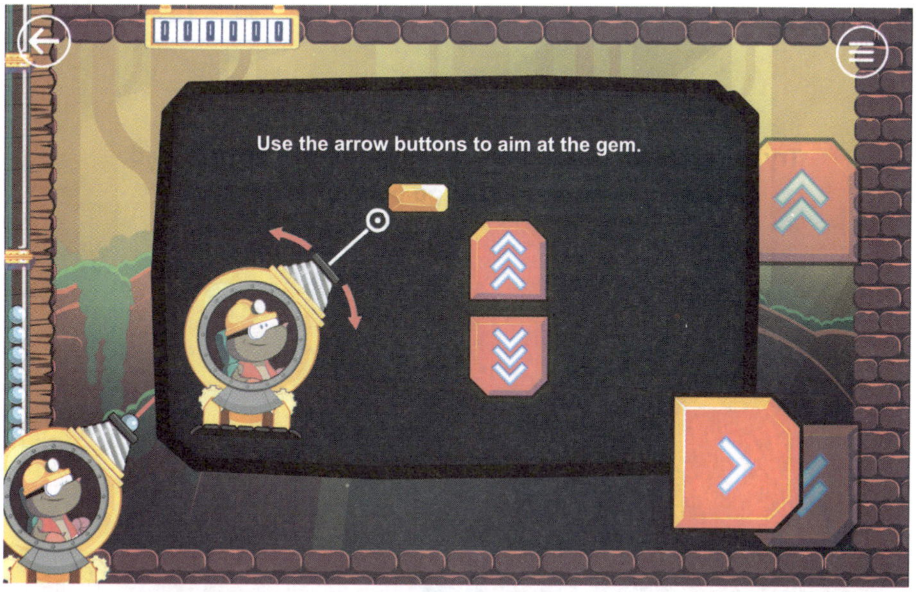

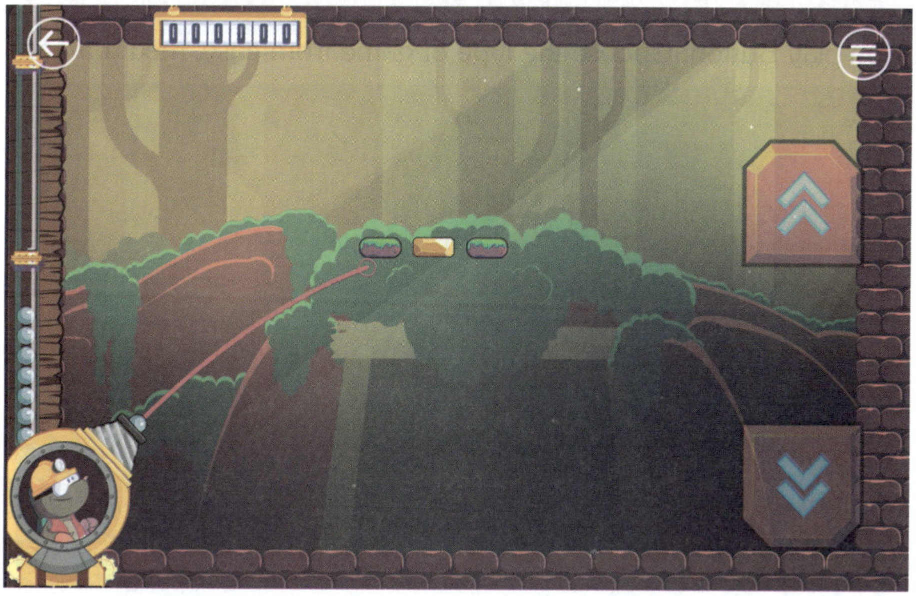

Hit and Play this wonderful game.

Game 2: https://www.abcya.com/games/tangrams

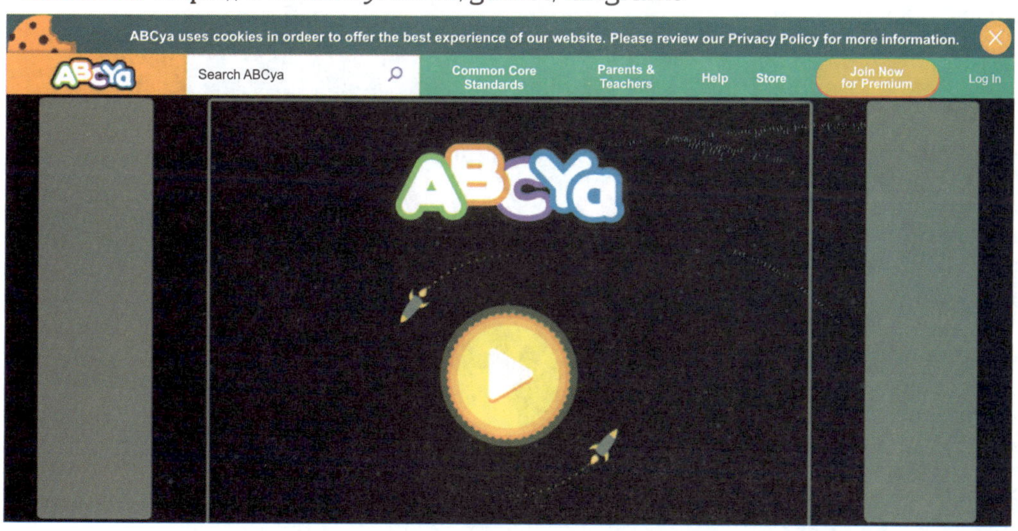

Game 2
in Action

Scan QR Code

1. Click on play button.

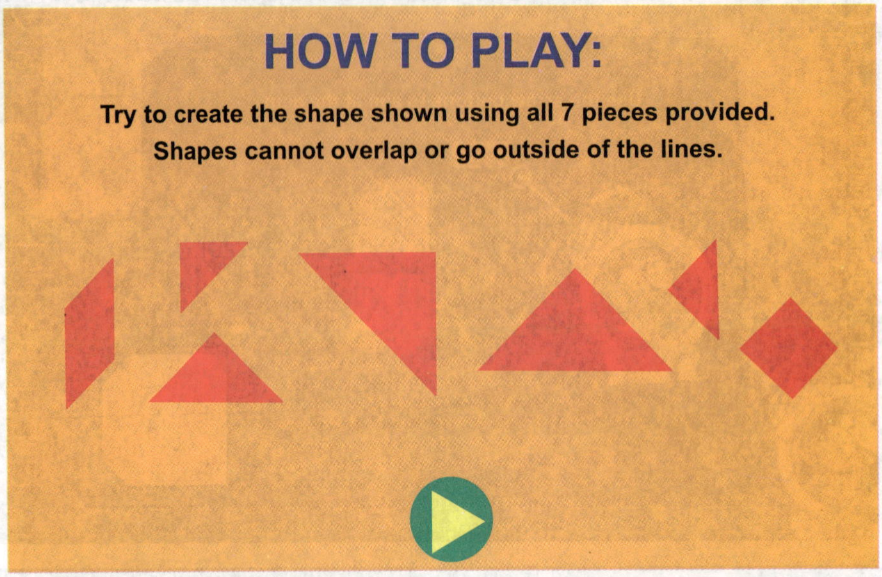

2. Again Click on play Button. Choose the type of game from easy, medium and hard.

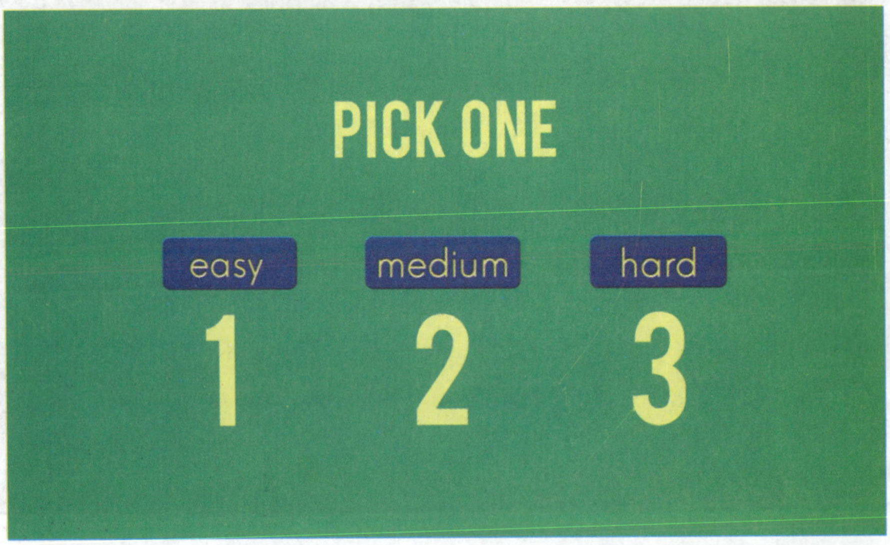

3. Choose the one which are unlocked.

4. Now drag the geometrical shapes on the image.

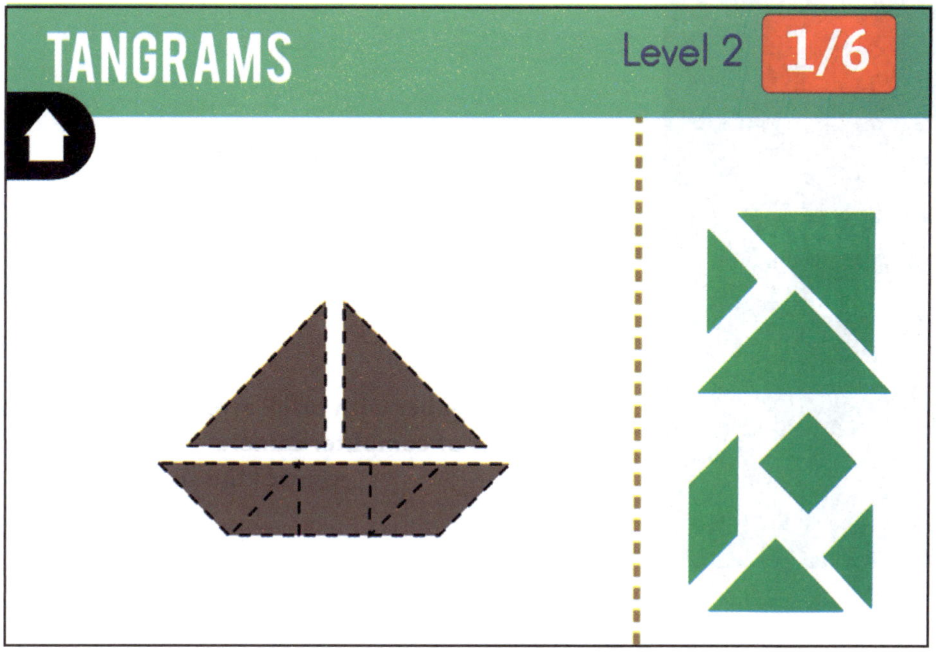

Enjoy Playing !!!

Game 3: Paint with fun

Visit the website: http://ganpaint-demo.vizhub.ai/

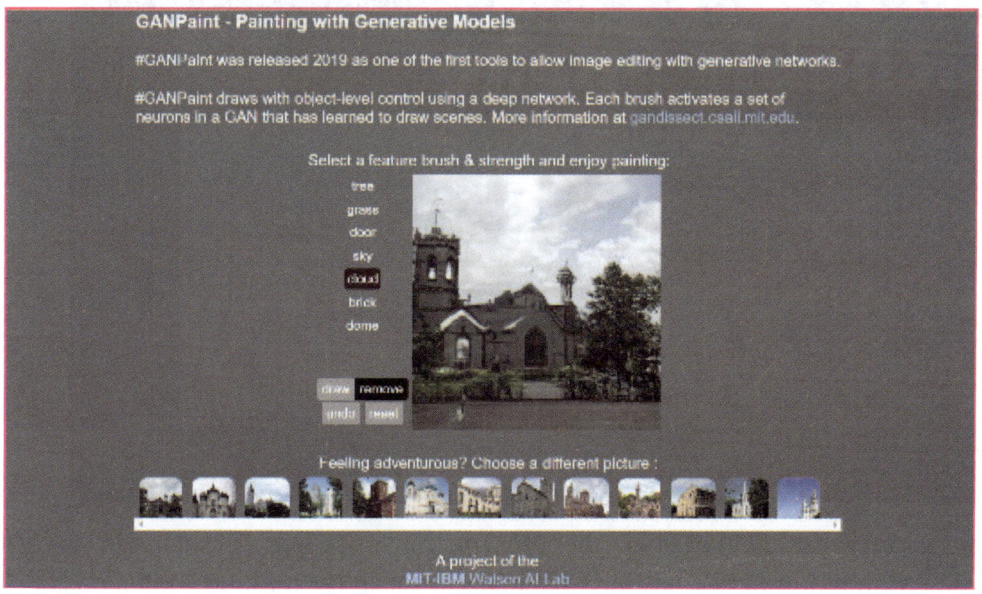

Treasure Link
Paint with Fun in Action

Scan QR Code

You can choose the painting and paint as per your need basis. You can draw or remove the feature using the buttons near the image.

Game 4: Teachable Snake Fun Game

Visit the website: https://teachable-snake.netlify.app/

Play the above game and observe how the snake moves.

The green box will move and when it will touch the yellow box, then the green box will thereby increase its size.

In summary, Computer Vision is a fascinating field that helps machines see and also helps us understand , the world around us. It has a huge impact on various aspects of our lives, making things easier, safer, and more efficient. By learning about Computer Vision, we can better appreciate how technology can see the world and assist us in many incredible ways.

LET'S REHASH

1. **Computer Vision (CV):** A field of AI that enables machines to interpret and understand the visual world.
2. **Real-Life Examples of CV:** Face recognition on phones and object detection fitted in self-driving cars.
3. **Capture Process:** Cameras and sensors capture the image for the computer to process.
4. **Understanding Images:** Computers process images by analyzing edges, shapes, and colors.
5. **Identification Process:** Machines compare captured images with pre-stored data to recognize objects.
6. **Steps in CV:** Detecting, processing, extracting features, understanding images, and making decisions.
7. **Detecting Images:** Computers use cameras and visual sensors to capture visuals like a smartphone taking selfies.
8. **Processing Images:** Computers analyze patterns in images to recognize objects.
9. **Feature Extraction:** The computer identifies key features in images like eyes, nose, and mouth in a face.
10. **Understanding:** The computer uses algorithms to interpret the features and decide what the image represents.
11. **Decision Making:** Once the image is understood, the computer takes actions, such as unlocking a phone.
12. **Face Recognition:** CV can identify people by recognizing facial features.
13. **Object Detection:** CV helps most of the machines identify and also categorize, objects like cars, people, and obstacles.
14. **Image Search:** Uploading a photo to find similar images, such as using Google Image Search.
15. **Augmented Reality (AR):** CV enables digital elements to be added to real-world images, like in Pokémon GO.
16. **Smartphones:** CV enhances the face recognition for unlocking devices securely.
17. **Self-Driving Cars:** CV helps in detecting roads, cars, and pedestrians for safe driving.
18. **Healthcare:** CV aids doctors in analyzing medical images like X-rays and MRIs.
19. **Industrial Uses:** CV helps in quality control by inspecting products for defects in factories.
20. **Education:** CV can well support visually impaired students and create interactive learning experiences with augmented reality.

To Solve Multiple Choice Questions Online

Scan QR Code and Check Your Score

EXERCISE

(A) Multiple Choice Questions with Answers

1. **What is Computer Vision?**
   (a) Teaching computers to type (b) Teaching computers to see and understand images
   (c) Teaching computers to speak (d) Teaching to sing a song
2. **What is the first step in computer vision?**
   (a) Making decisions (b) Processing the image
   (c) Detecting the image (d) Explore the image
3. **Which devices are used to capture images in CV?**
   (a) Microphones (b) Cameras and sensors
   (c) Keyboards (d) Observation
4. **What is feature extraction in CV?**
   (a) Identifying key parts of an image (b) Making decisions from images
   (c) Capturing the image (d) Identifying pattern
5. **Which of the following is an example of CV in action?**
   (a) Speech recognition (b) Face recognition on smartphones
   (c) Text messaging (d) Dancing on stage
6. **What does CV do in self-driving cars?**
   (a) Teaches driving skills (b) Recognizes roads and obstacles
   (c) Controls the car's engine (d) Identify objects
7. **What is used to process images in CV?**
   (a) Cameras (b) Sensors
   (c) Algorithms (d) Survey
8. **What type of games use CV technology?**
   (a) Puzzle games (b) Eye-tracking games
   (c) Racing games (d) AR games
9. **What role does CV play in healthcare?**
   (a) Assisting in medical image analysis (b) Prescribing medicines
   (c) Conducting surgeries (d) Identify criminals

10. Which of the following uses CV for entertainment?
(a) Medical diagnosis
(b) Augmented Reality games like Pokémon GO
(c) Teaching students
(d) Singing songs

11. What technology is used to process and understand images in CV?
(a) Sensors
(b) Algorithms
(c) Microchips
(d) Camera

12. What does AR stand for?
(a) Artificial Reality
(b) Augmented Reality
(c) Applied Reality
(d) Application in reality

13. How does CV improve security in smartphones?
(a) By capturing photos
(b) Through face recognition
(c) By detecting fingerprints
(d) Through pattern recordings

14. What is the purpose of feature extraction in CV?
(a) To unlock a phone
(b) To identify important parts of an image
(c) To store data
(d) To use data

15. How does CV help in self-driving cars?
(a) By detecting traffic lights and road signs
(b) By playing music
(c) By changing tyres
(d) By changing speed

16. In which industry does CV assist in quality control?
(a) Entertainment
(b) Manufacturing
(c) Banking
(d) Education

17. What does CV do in AR games like Pokémon GO?
(a) Makes 3D characters
(b) Overlays digital images onto the real world
(c) Teaches coding
(d) Teaches movement

18. What does CV help doctors analyse?
(a) Blood pressure
(b) X-rays and MRIs
(c) Heartbeats
(d) Recording heart beats

19. What process follows feature extraction in CV?
(a) Capturing the image
(b) Understanding the image
(c) Detecting obstacles
(d) Recording the image

20. What is an example of CV improving safety?
(a) Monitoring assembly lines
(b) Detecting suspicious activities through surveillance
(c) Helping in interactive learning
(d) Capturing data

ANSWERS

1.	(b)	2.	(c)	3.	(b)	4.	(a)	5.	(b)
6.	(b)	7.	(c)	8.	(b)	9.	(a)	10.	(b)
11.	(b)	12.	(b)	13.	(b)	14.	(b)	15.	(a)
16.	(b)	17.	(b)	18.	(b)	19.	(b)	20.	(b)

(B) Fill in the Blanks with Answers

1. Computer Vision (CV) helps machines to understand the ________ world.

Ans. visual

2. The first step in CV is ________ the image.

Ans. detecting

3. CV uses ________ and sensors to capture images.

Ans. cameras

4. ________ extraction is identifying key parts of an image.

Ans. Feature

5. Self-driving cars use CV to recognize ________ and pedestrians.

Ans. obstacles

6. CV uses ________ to completely process images and understand them.

Ans. algorithms

7. Augmented Reality (AR) adds ________ images to real-world environments.

Ans. digital

8. Face recognition in smartphones is a key example of ________.

Ans. Computer Vision

9. In healthcare, a CV helps doctors analyze ________ and MRIs.

Ans. X-rays

10. CV can improve the quality control process by inspecting products for ________.

Ans. defects

11. The ________ is used to capture shortlisted images before processing.

Ans. camera

12. ________ recognition is a major application of CV for unlocking phones.

Ans. Face

13. CV helps machines to fully recognize edges, ________, and colors in images.

Ans. shapes

14. CV is used in ________ to identify suspicious activities through surveillance.

Ans. security

15. AR games like Pokémon GO use CV to place all digital characters into the ________ world.

Ans. real

(c) Short Questions with Answers

1. **What is Computer Vision (CV)?**

Ans. CV is a field in AI that enables machines to fully interpret and understand visual data like images and videos.

2. **What devices are used in CV to capture images?**

Ans. Cameras and sensors.

3. **How does feature extraction work in CV?**

Ans. The computer identifies key parts of an image, such as eyes, nose, and mouth, in a face.

4. **What role does CV play in self-driving cars?**

Ans. CV helps the car detect roads, obstacles, pedestrians, and other vehicles to navigate safely.

5. **What is an example of CV in smartphones?**

Ans. Face recognition for unlocking the phone.

6. **How does CV work in Augmented Reality (AR)?**

Ans. It overlays digital elements onto all the real-world images captured through a camera.

7. **What is the importance of algorithms in CV?**

Ans. Algorithms process and interpret features in images to help machines understand what they are really seeing.

8. **How does CV improve healthcare?**

Ans. CV helps doctors analyze medical images like X-rays and MRIs for better diagnosis.

9. **What is an example of CV in industrial applications?**

Ans. CV is used for quality control by thoroughly inspecting products on assembly lines for defects.

10. **What does CV do in given security systems?**

Ans. CV monitors surveillance cameras to detect suspicious activities and enhance safety.

ACTIVITY-BASED QUESTIONS

1. **Activity:** Take a series of photos of common objects (e.g., car, tree, chair) and try using an online image recognition tool towards identify them. Document how accurately the tool recognizes each object.
2. **Activity:** Explore an Augmented Reality (AR) app or a game such as Pokémon GO or Roblo x, and describe how digital objects interact with the real-world environment through your camera.

TEACHER'S NOTES

4.1 Introduction

- CV enables machines to "see" and interpret visuals.

Activity: Ask students—what gadgets can "see" (camera, scanner, phone).

4.2 What is Computer Vision

- Machines capture, understand, and identify images.

Activity: Show a blurred image and ask students to guess it—relate to how AI identifies.

4.3 How CV Works

- Steps: Detect → Process → Extract Features → Understand → Act.

Activity: Play a short video of self-driving cars; pause to explain each step.

4.4 Examples of CV in Action

- Face recognition, object detection, image search, augmented reality.

Activity: Use phone's Face Unlock or AR filter for a live demo.

4.5 Importance of CV

- Improves safety, healthcare, quality control, and entertainment.

Activity: Students draw a simple flowchart showing "How CV helps people".

CHAPTER 5

AI GAMES

AI Games in Action

Scan QR Code

OBJECTIVES

TOPICS TO BE COVERED

- Introduction to AI Games
- Apps to Understand AI and Machine Learning
- About AI
- Ten Interesting Facts of AI

5.1 Introduction to AI Games

AI games are video games that use artificial intelligence to make the games more challenging. Students enjoy such games because it appears as if are actually playing it with a real-life person. They in these games, the computer-controlled characters, called NPCs (non-playable characters), can think and make decisions just like a real person would. This makes the game more challenging because the characters can adapt to what the player is doing. For example, in a chess game, an AI opponent can plan its moves to try and win against the player. AI also helps to create new game levels and challenges, making sure each time you play, the game feels different and more exciting. AI games offer a more interactive and enjoyable experience for players of all ages.

5.2 Apps to Understand AI and Machine Learning

There are some of the apps to help you get an in-depth understanding of AI and machine learning. These are as follows:

- **Pika:** A cool camera app for kids. They can take pictures of colors, and the app teaches robots to recognize those colors.
- **Machine Learning for Kids:** This app lets kids work with Scratch (a coding platform) and spreadsheets. They can teach machines using pictures, and parents can track their progress.
- **Dalton Learning Lab:** It offers free tools for parents and kids to learn AI and machine learning, including Scratch, without needing to sign up.
- **Kano Computing:** Kids can build their own computers and program them to do tasks. There's also a guide to help them along the way.
- **VIPER:** A game from Wonderville that makes learning about machine learning fun. In the game, kids program a robot to explore Europe.

- **Azure Machine Learning:** A tool to help organize and test machine learning models. It can even help build systems that make recommendations, like what to watch next on TV.
- **Caffe:** An open-source tool for deep learning. It's especially good for tasks like recognizing images and breaking them down into parts.
- **CNTK:** A deep learning tool from Microsoft. It helps computers learn step by step, like connecting the dots in a graph.
- **IBM Watson:** A super smart computer that can answer questions like a human. It uses AI to give the best possible answers.
- **PyBrain:** A Python-based tool for learning about machine learning. It's great for beginners and advanced learners to create smart systems.
- **Scikit-Learn:** A tool for learning machine learning in Python, useful for understanding patterns in data, creating graphs, and making predictions.
- **Swift AI:** A tool for developing neural networks and deep learning algorithms, mainly used on Mac computers.
- **Tensor Flow:** A tool created by Google to help computers learn like humans. It's great for deep learning and handling big math problems.

FUN.AI ACTIVITY

Treasure Link
Start chatting with Viper
in Action

Scan QR Code

Scan the website: https://www.talkie-ai.com/chat
Start chatting with Viper.

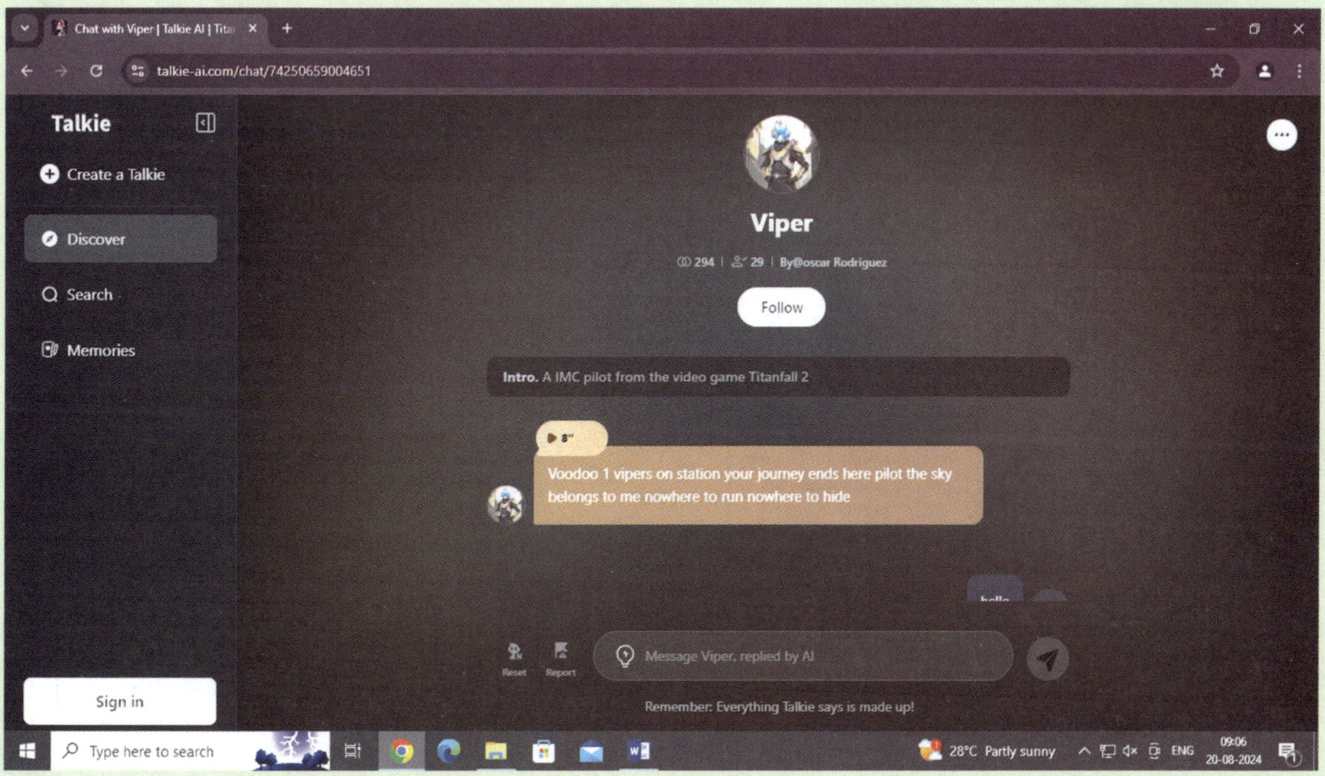

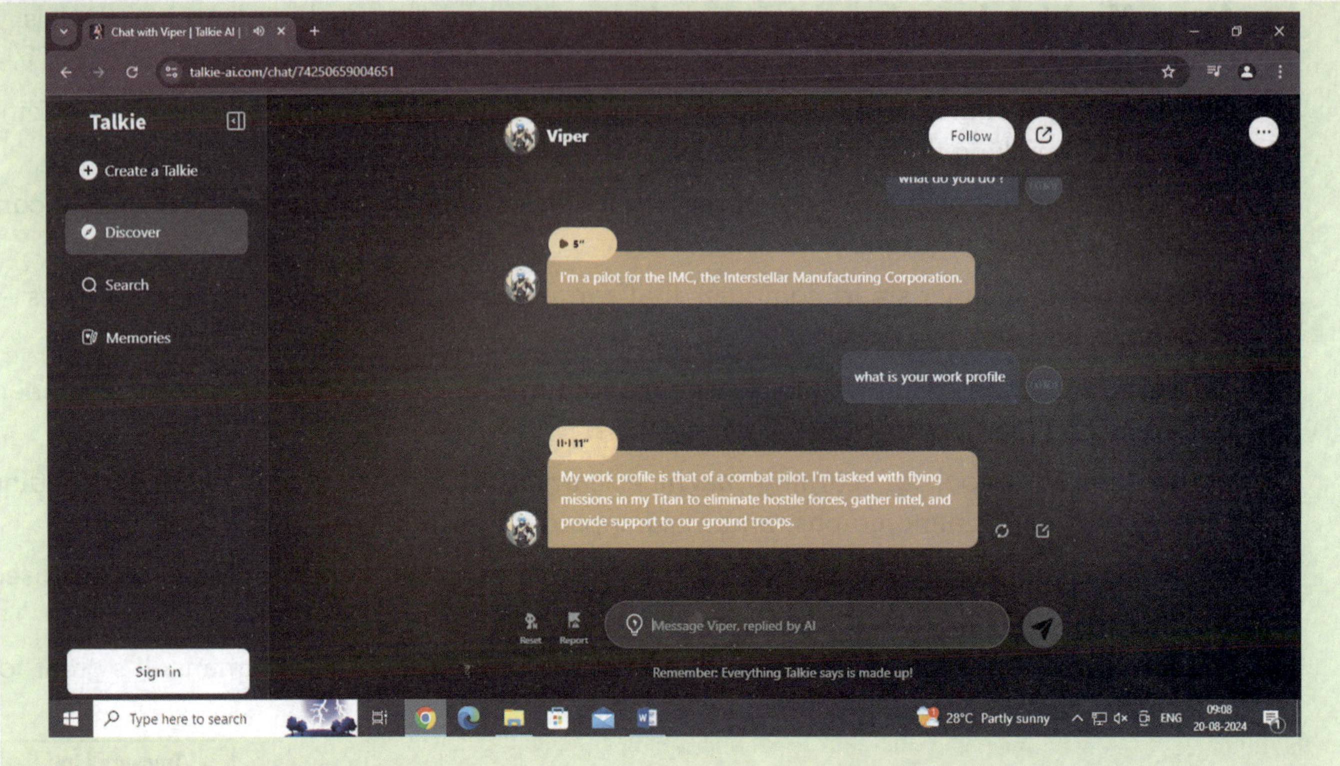

5.3 About AI

Machine learning is an artificial intelligence technique that has seen new developments by creating new algorithms which imitate or support human behaviour or decision-making capabilities like Apple's Siri, or the email servers which eliminate junk or spam emails. Before talking about the facts of AI, let us watch some videos to understand facts about Artificial intelligence:

WATCH VIDEOS

1. **Treasure Link**
What is Artificial Intelligence Exactly?
in Action
Scan QR Code

2. **Treasure Link**
What is Artificial Intelligence?
in Action
Scan QR Code

3. **Treasure Link**
Jimmy Meets Sophia the Human-Like Robot
in Action
Scan QR Code

4. **Treasure Link**
Interview With the Lifelike Robot Named Sophia
in Action
Scan QR Code

5. **Treasure Link**
AI vs Machine Learning vs Deep Learning
in Action
Scan QR Code

FUN.AI ACTIVITY

Treasure Link
Teachable Snake in Action
Scan QR Code

Scan the QR code and Visit the website: https://teachable-snake.netlify.app/

Play the game and observe how the snake moves.

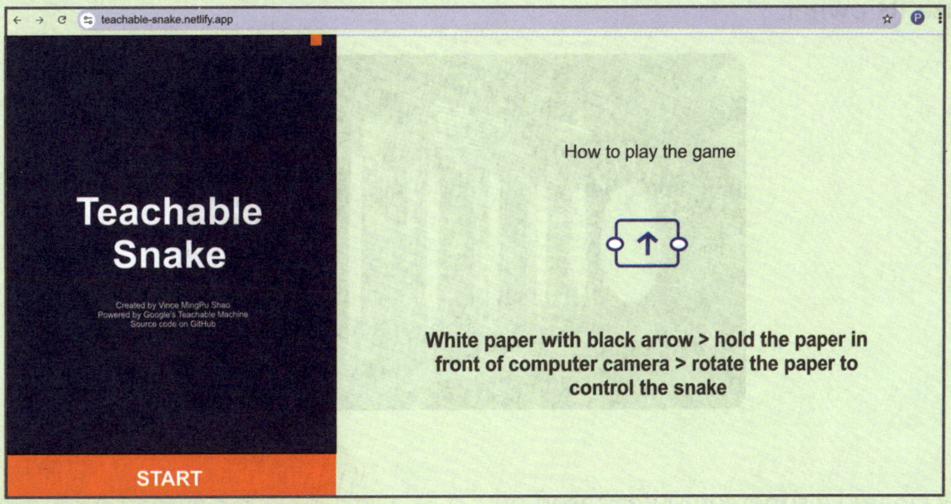

The green box will move and when it touches the yellow box, then the green box increases its size.

5.4 Ten Interesting Facts of AI

1. **Google's AI-Powered Predictions:** Using unknown location data from smartphones, Google Maps (Maps) can analyse the speed of movement of traffic at any given time. And, with its acquisition of crowd sourced traffic app Waze in 2013, Maps can more easily incorporate user-reported traffic incidents like construction and accidents.

2. With machine learning and language recognition, it is expected that 85% of telephonic customer service jobs will be performed by computers and will not need human interaction.
3. It is a fact that with increased intelligence and ability to perform tasks with accuracy, it is predicted that over the next few years around three million workers will be reporting to or will be supervised by "Robot-bosses".
4. Sony created a robotic dog called Aibo. It is one of its first toys that could be bought and played with. It could express emotions and could also recognize its owner.

Treasure Link
Five things you really need to know about AI in Action

Scan QR Code

5. IBM has created a supercomputer based on AI, called Watson. Watson could understand questions in most of the common languages and has the ability to attend to those questions in real time.
6. Autonomous vehicles will be in market soon. The knight rider can become a reality in the next 2-3 years or less. These cars are based on the artificial intelligence that can recognize the driving conditions and adapt the behaviour. These cars are under testing and are likely to be launched soon.
7. Researchers at the University of Stanford have built a machine learning algorithm that can predict your death with as good as 90% accuracy.
8. Nautilus, a self-learning supercomputer can foretell your future. This is the same robot that located Osama Bin Laden and gained worldwide fame. It can calculate its predictions from the information provided to it.
9. A new methodology has been developed by roboticist that can create an image of your thoughts using an FMRI scanner. The AI is designed to construct an

Scooby-Doo Quest

Q. Match the following

1. Sony	A. Waston
2. Hanson Robotics	B. Aibo
3. IBM	C. Sophia
4. Google Maps	D. Nautilus
5. Super Computer	E. Waze.

Answers. 1. (B) 2. (C) 3. (A) 4. (E) 5. (D)

W'e Tech Planet

NAUTILUS SUPERCOMPUTER

Can predict future events

Nautilus is a supercomputer with the ability to make predictions about future events. It is like a self-learning supercomputer that provides results of future events based on news articles and information that are fed into it.

image from your brain and compare it with other pictures, received from volunteers. FMRI scanner is a kind of magnetic resonance imaging scanner.

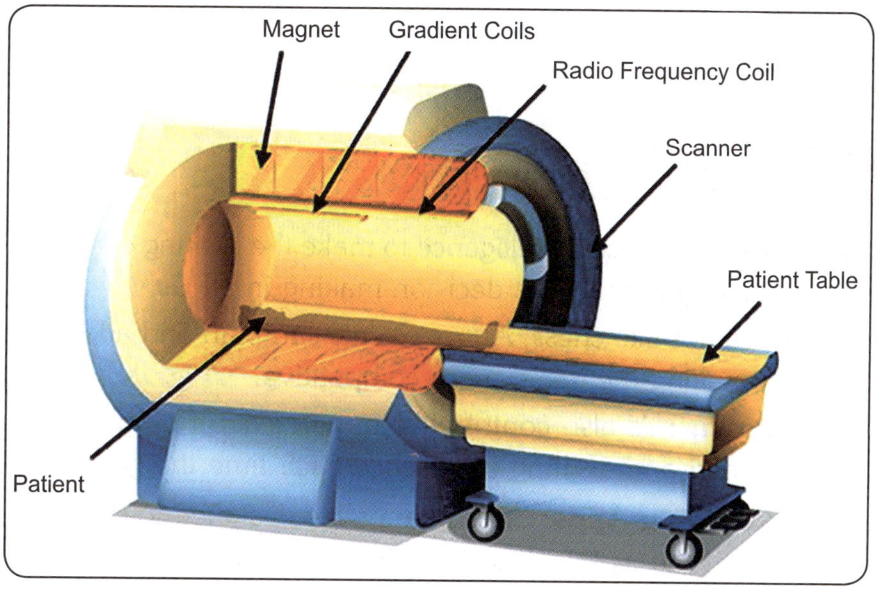

FMRI scanner

10. Sophia, a life-like humanoid has gained guaranteed citizenship of Saudi Arabia. She was created by Dr. David Hanson, founder of Hanson Robotics. Sophia uses artificial intelligence, visual data processing and facial recognition. Sophia also imitates human gestures and facial expressions and is able to answer certain questions and make simple conversations on predefined topics.

Sophia giving Interview

LET'S REHASH

1. **AI Games:** AI games use artificial intelligence to make the gaming experience more challenging and realistic by simulating human-like decision-making in NPCs.
2. **AI in Chess:** In AI games like chess, AI opponents can plan and adapt their moves based on the player's actions, making the game more competitive.
3. **AI Game Development:** AI also contributes to the creation of new levels and challenges in games, ensuring a varied and exciting experience each time the game is played.
4. **AI and Machine Learning Apps:** Several apps are designed to help children understand AI and machine learning, such as Pika and Machine Learning for Kids.
5. **Pika App:** Pika is a camera app that teaches kids about colours and allows them to train robots through photography.
6. **Machine Learning for Kids App:** This app provides tools like Scratch and Spreadsheets to help parents track their children's progress in teaching machines through image selection.
7. **Dalton Learning Lab:** Offers tools for parents to help their children learn about AI and machine learning, with free Scratch options.
8. **Kano Computing:** An app that allows kids to build and program their own computers, offering guidance throughout the learning process.
9. **VIPER Game:** Wonderville's VIPER game teaches kids about machine learning by having them program a robot to explore Europe.
10. **Azure Machine Learning:** A cloud-based service that allows users to organize predictive models, test machine learning models, and create recommender systems.
11. **Caffe Framework:** An open-source deep learning framework designed for image segmentation and classification.
12. **CNTK:** Microsoft's deep learning toolkit that describes neural networks as a series of computational steps via a directed graph.
13. **IBM Watson:** A question answering machine that uses AI to replicate human-like abilities to respond to questions optimally.
14. **PyBrain:** An open-source, modular machine learning library entirely based on Python, designed for both beginners and researchers.
15. **Scikit-Learn:** A Python-based framework for machine learning, useful for data mining, analysis, and visualization.

16. **Swift AI:** A deep learning and neural network library for Swift, enabling developers to create neural networks and algorithms.
17. **TensorFlow:** A Google-developed framework for deep learning, neural networks, and machine learning research.
18. **AI in Daily Life:** AI is present in everyday applications like Siri, email spam filters, and more, imitating human behaviour.
19. **Interesting AI Facts:** Facts about AI include Google Maps using AI for traffic predictions, and robots like Sony's Aibo, which can recognize emotions.
20. **AI in Future:** The future of AI includes developments like autonomous vehicles, robot bosses, and AI predicting human death with high accuracy.

To Solve Multiple Choice Questions Online

Scan QR Code and Check Your Score

EXERCISE

(A) Multiple Choice Questions with Answers

1. What does NPC stand for in AI games?

(a) Non-Person Character (b) Non-Playable Character

(c) Non-Player Control (d) Non-Play Character

2. Which AI app allows kids to teach machines through image selection?

(a) Pika (b) VIPER

(c) Machine Learning for Kids (d) Helo

3. What is the main purpose of AI in games like chess?

(a) To create new levels (b) To adapt moves based on player actions

(c) To provide hints to players (d) To teach concentration

4. Which app allows children to develop and program their own computers?

(a) VIPER (b) Kano Computing

(c) Swift AI (d) Helo

5. What type of service is Azure Machine Learning?

(a) A desktop application (b) A cloud-based service

(c) A mobile app (d) Social media app

6. **Which of the following is an open-source deep learning framework?**
   (a) Caffe (b) Scikit-Learn
   (c) TensorFlow (d) Pie
7. **What does IBM Watson do?**
   (a) It plays video games (b) It answers questions using AI
   (c) It predicts traffic conditions (d) It predicts weather
8. **Which AI fact relates to predicting death with 90% accuracy?**
   (a) Google's AI-Powered Predictions (b) Autonomous Vehicles
   (c) Stanford's machine learning algorithm (d) Tensor flow
9. **What is the VIPER game about?**
   (a) Racing cars (b) Exploring Europe with a programmed robot
   (c) Building computers (d) Learning sports
10. **Who developed the CNTK deep learning toolkit?**
   (a) Google (b) Microsoft
   (c) IBM (d) Dell
11. **Which AI app is designed for image classification?**
   (a) PyBrain (b) TensorFlow
   (c) Caffe (d) Pie
12. **Which AI app helps with deep learning and neural networks in Swift?**
   (a) Swift AI (b) Scikit-Learn
   (c) TensorFlow (d) Pie
13. **Which AI tool was used to locate Osama Bin Laden?**
   (a) Nautilus (b) Aibo
   (c) Sophia (d) Rainbow
14. **Which app provides free Scratch options for learning AI?**
   (a) Dalton Learning Lab (b) Pika
   (c) Pybrain (d) IT lab
15. **What does Scikit-Learn help with?**
   (a) Game development (b) Data analysis and visualization
   (c) Building robots (d) Data Mining
16. **Which AI fact relates to Google Maps?**
   (a) AI for traffic predictions (b) AI for medical diagnosis
   (c) AI for autonomous vehicles (d) AI for Tourism
17. **What is TensorFlow primarily used for?**
   (a) Creating video games
   (b) Conducting deep learning and neural network research
   (c) Monitoring traffic
   (d) Finding routes
18. **Which app allows parents to track their child's progress in machine learning?**
   (a) VIPER (b) Machine Learning for Kids
   (c) Pika (d) Pie

19. What is a primary function of the AI app Watson?

(a) To assist in machine learning tasks (b) To answer questions in real-time

(c) To predict future events (d) To predict weather

20. Which AI-based fact is related to self-driving cars?

(a) They are currently available in the market

(b) They can recognize and adapt to driving conditions

(c) They are operated by humans

(d) They cannot judge

ANSWERS

1.	(b)	2.	(c)	3.	(b)	4.	(b)	5.	(b)
6.	(a)	7.	(b)	8.	(c)	9.	(b)	10.	(b)
11.	(c)	12.	(a)	13.	(a)	14.	(a)	15.	(b)
16.	(a)	17.	(b)	18.	(b)	19.	(b)	20.	(b)

(B) Fill in the Blanks with Answers

1. AI games make use of __________ to enhance the gameplay experience.

Ans. artificial intelligence

2. __________are computer-controlled characters in AI games that adapt to player actions.

Ans. NPCs

3. The __________ app allows kids to photograph objects and help robots learn about colours.

Ans. Pika

4. __________ is a cloud-based service for organizing predictive models and testing machine learning models.

Ans. Azure Machine Learning

5. __________ is an open-source deep learning framework that focuses on image segmentation and classification.

Ans. Caffe

6. __________ describes neural networks through computational graphs.

Ans. CNTK

7. __________ is known for its question-answering capabilities and real-time processing.

Ans. IBM Watson

8. __________is an open-source machine learning library that is completely Python-based.

Ans. PyBrain

9. __________is a machine learning framework used for data mining, data analysis, and data visualization.

Ans. Scikit-Learn

10. ______________AI is a library for creating neural networks and deep learning algorithms in Swift.

Ans. Swift

11. ______________ was developed by Google for deep learning and machine learning research.

Ans. Tensor Flow

12. Machine learning and ______________are expected to replace many telephonic customer service jobs.

Ans. language recognition

13. ______________is a robotic dog that can express emotions and recognize its owner.

Ans. Sony's Aibo

14. ______________is a life-like humanoid robot granted citizenship in Saudi Arabia.

Ans. Sophia

15. ______________is a self-learning supercomputer that can predict future events.

Ans. Nautilus

16. ______________uses AI-powered predictions to analyse traffic conditions.

Ans. Google Maps

17. ______________is a game introduced by Wonderville to make machine learning interesting for kids.

Ans. VIPER

18. ______________Lab offers tools to help parents with AI and machine learning.

Ans. Dalton Learning

19. ______________Computing enables kids to build and program their own computers.

Ans. Kano

20. ______________provides tools for kids to teach machines through image selection.

Ans. Machine Learning for Kids

(C) Short Questions with Answers

1. What are AI games?

Ans. AI games are video games that use artificial intelligence to make gameplay more challenging by having computer-controlled characters (NPCs) make decisions and adapt to the player's actions.

2. Name an app that allows kids to photograph objects and teach robots about colours.

Ans. Pika

3. What is the function of Azure Machine Learning?

Ans. Azure Machine Learning is a cloud-based service for organizing predictive models, testing machine learning models, and creating recommender systems.

4. **Which deep learning framework is designed for image segmentation and classification?**

Ans. Caffe

5. **What does CNTK stand for?**

Ans. Computational Network Toolkit

6. **What is the main purpose of IBM Watson?**

Ans. IBM Watson is designed for question-answering and can process questions in multiple languages in real time.

7. **Which library is known for data mining, data analysis, and data visualization in Python?**

Ans. Scikit-Learn

8. **What is the main feature of the Swift AI library?**

Ans. Swift AI is used for creating neural networks and deep learning algorithms in Swift.

9. **What technology is known for its ability to predict traffic conditions using smartphone data?**

Ans. Google Maps

10. **Which robot was granted citizenship by Saudi Arabia?**

Ans. Sophia

ACTIVITY-BASED QUESTIONS

1. Draw a simple game flowchart or storyboard to illustrate the gameplay and AI integration.
2. Explore and review educational AI apps to understand their features and potential for teaching AI concepts.
3. Identify the following device and write a brief explanation about them:

TEACHER'S NOTES

5.1. Introduction to AI Games

- AI makes games think and respond like humans.
- Used in Chess, Ludo, Quick Draw, etc.

Activity: Name games with computer opponents and discuss how they "think."

5.2. How AI Works in Games

- AI predicts moves and plans reactions.
- Uses pathfinding, decision trees, and learning.

Activity: Play a computer game (like Tic-Tac-Toe) and observe how it reacts.

5.3 Role of AI in Game Development

- Controls smart characters (NPCs).
- Builds realistic environments and adaptive levels.

Activity: Show a short gameplay video; discuss how AI makes it interesting.

5.4 Types of AI in Games

- Reactive: Immediate response (Pac-Man).
- Predictive: Guesses next move.
- Adaptive: Learns from play.
- Generative: Creates new levels/designs.

Activity: Show game screenshots and identify which AI type fits.

5.5 Popular AI-based Games

- Examples: Chess Engine, Quick Draw, Minecraft, AlphaGo, Candy Crush.

Activity: Play "Google Quick Draw" and discuss how AI guesses drawings.

5.6 Benefits of AI in Games

- Makes games fun, smart, and personalized.
- Saves time for developers.

Activity: Ask students: "What makes a game fun?" – link to AI's role.

5.7 Limitations of AI in Games

- Can be predictable or too difficult.
- Needs strong processing power.

Activity: Discuss games that feel "too easy" or "too hard" due to AI.

5.8 Future of AI in Gaming

- Combines AI with VR, voice, and gestures.
- AI will design new stories and experiences.

Activity: Students imagine and describe a future AI-based game.

LEARN WITH AI

Watch this Video and Learn What is AI in Action

Scan QR Code

FUN GAME: Play and see how AI works.

Affinelayer
in Action

Scan QR Code

1. Draw an image of cat and then click on 'process'. The model will draw a similar cat.

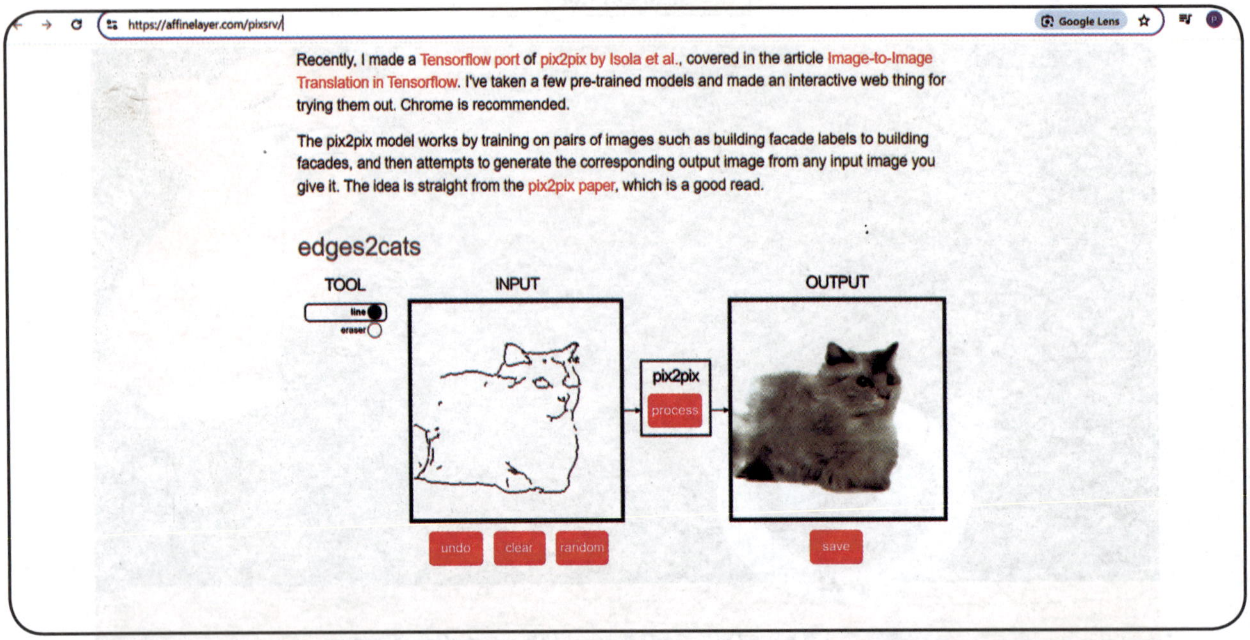

2. Scroll down.

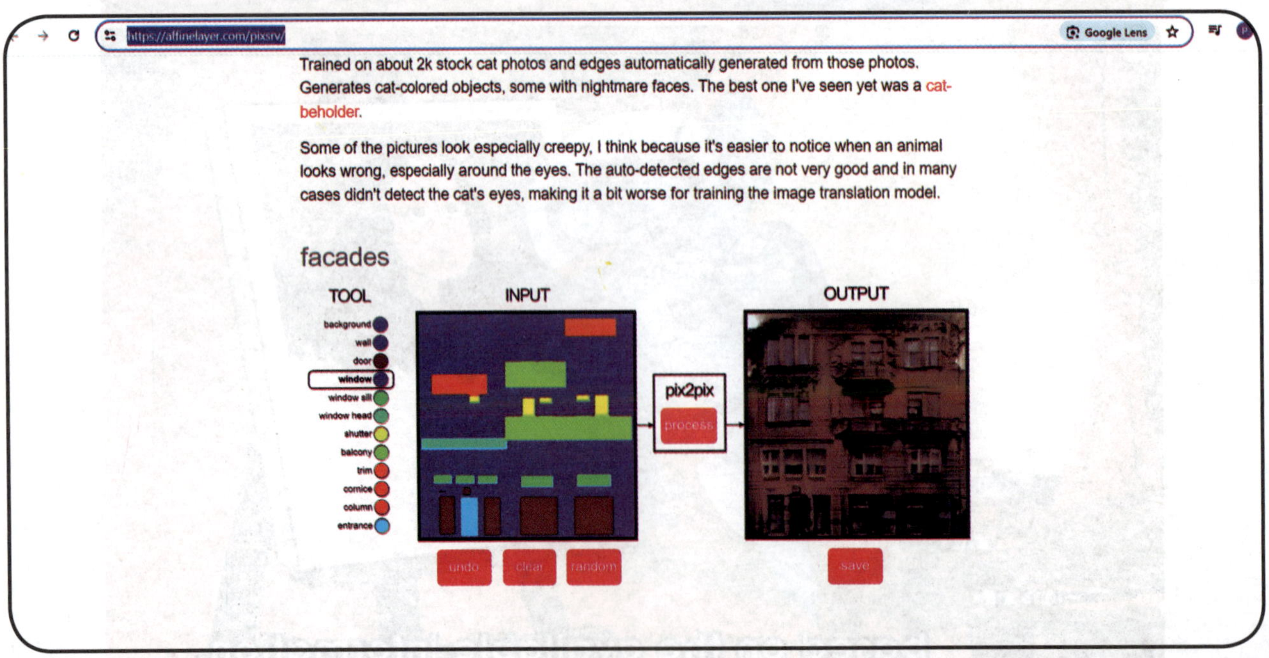

3. Make the changes in the input. Draw or clear picture of anything from the list. The output will show the same after you click on 'process'.

4. Scroll down.

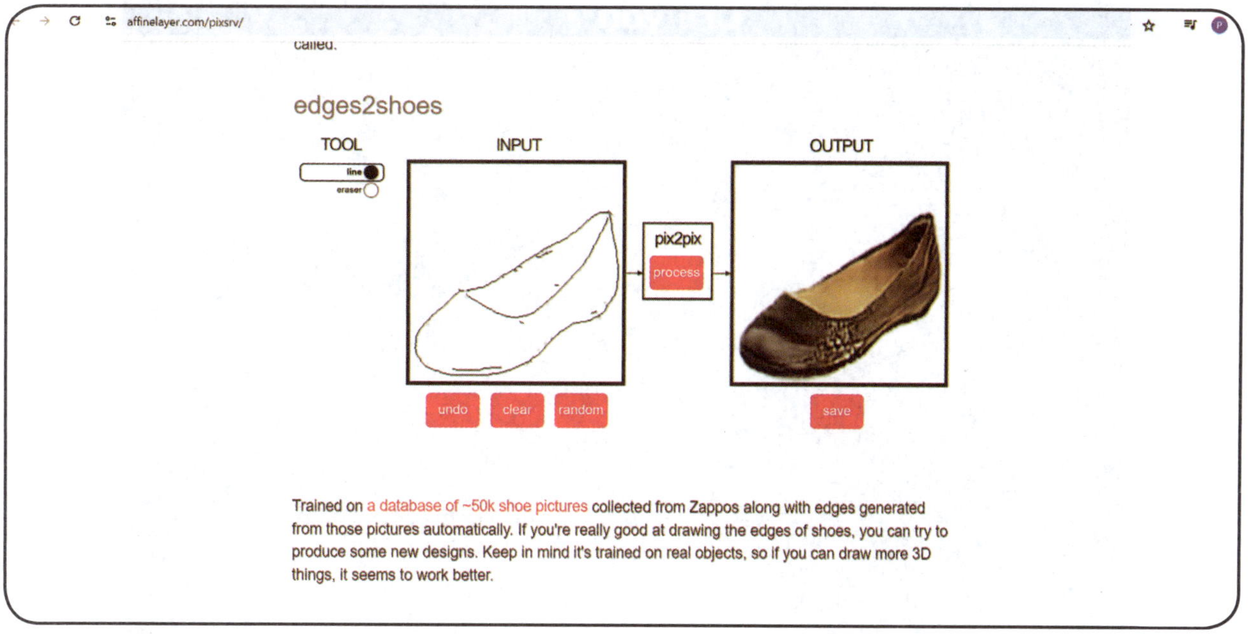

5. Draw the shape of the shoe and click on 'process". The same output will be displayed.
6. Scroll down.

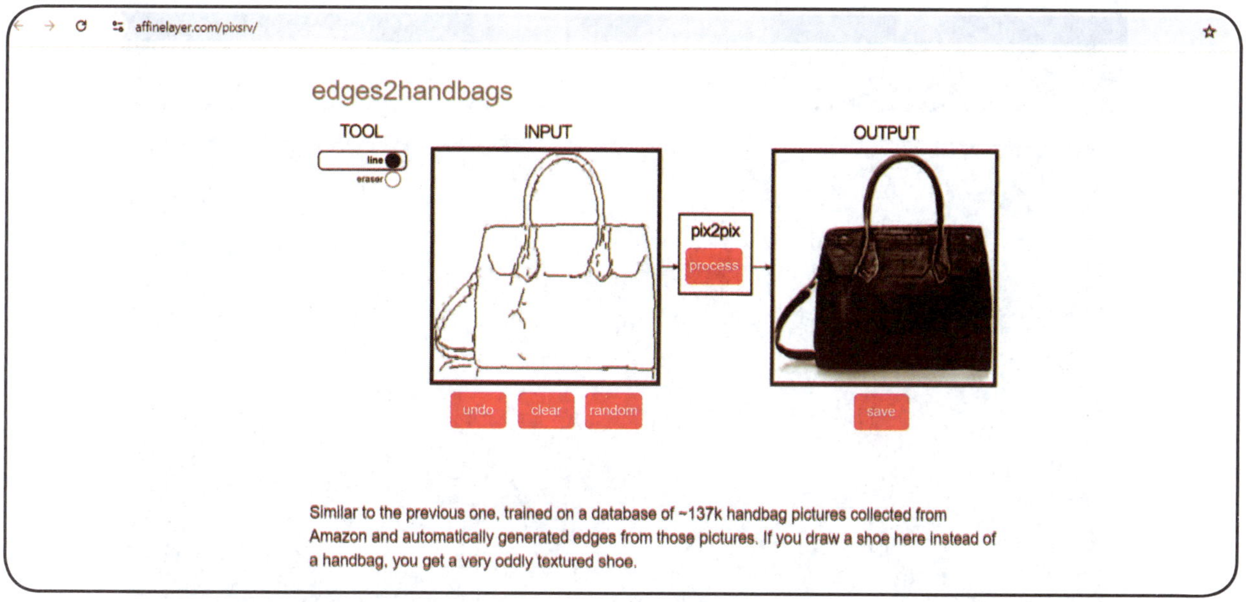

7. Draw the shape of the purse and click on 'process'. The same output will be displayed.

DRAW WITH AI:

Scan the QR Code and visit the site: https://www.craiyon.com/

1. Type the picture you want to draw. Like here I wrote a monkey climbing a tree. Click on 'Drawing' button. The image will be generated as shown below:

Craiyon: Draw With AI in Action

Scan QR Code

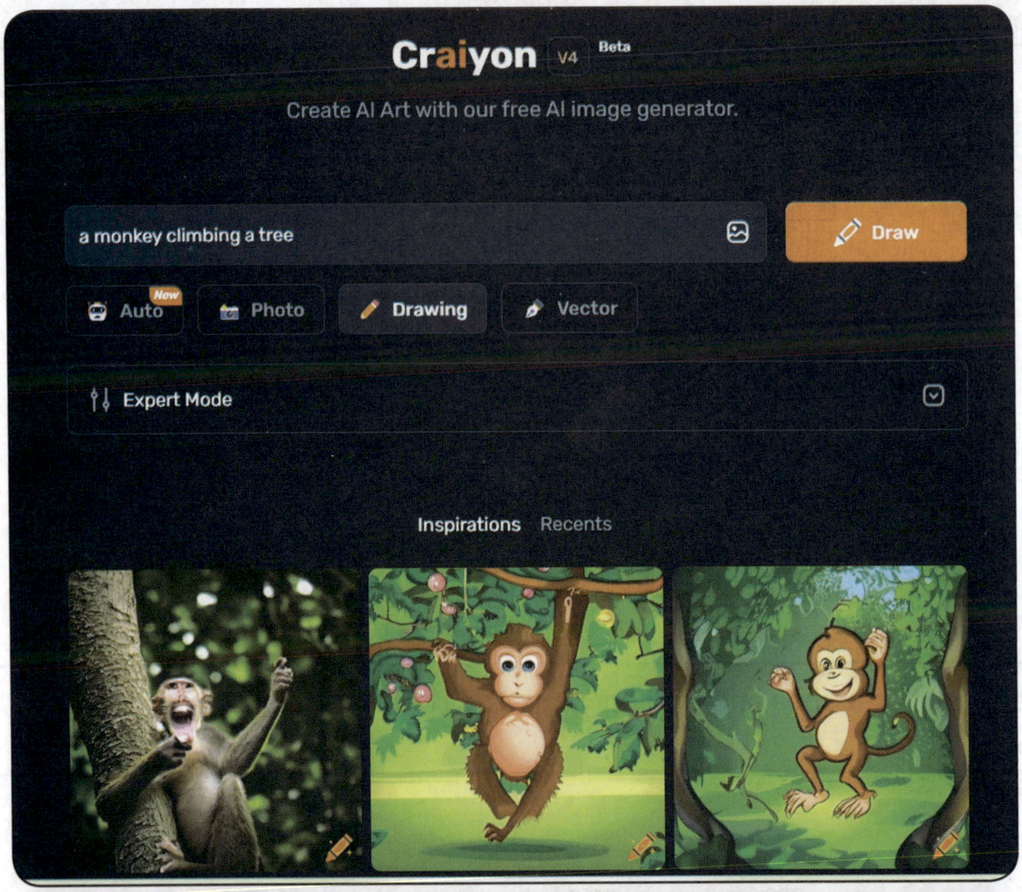
Craiyon V4 Beta
Create AI Art with our free AI image generator.
a monkey climbing a tree
Draw
Auto New
Photo
Drawing
Vector
Expert Mode
Inspirations Recents

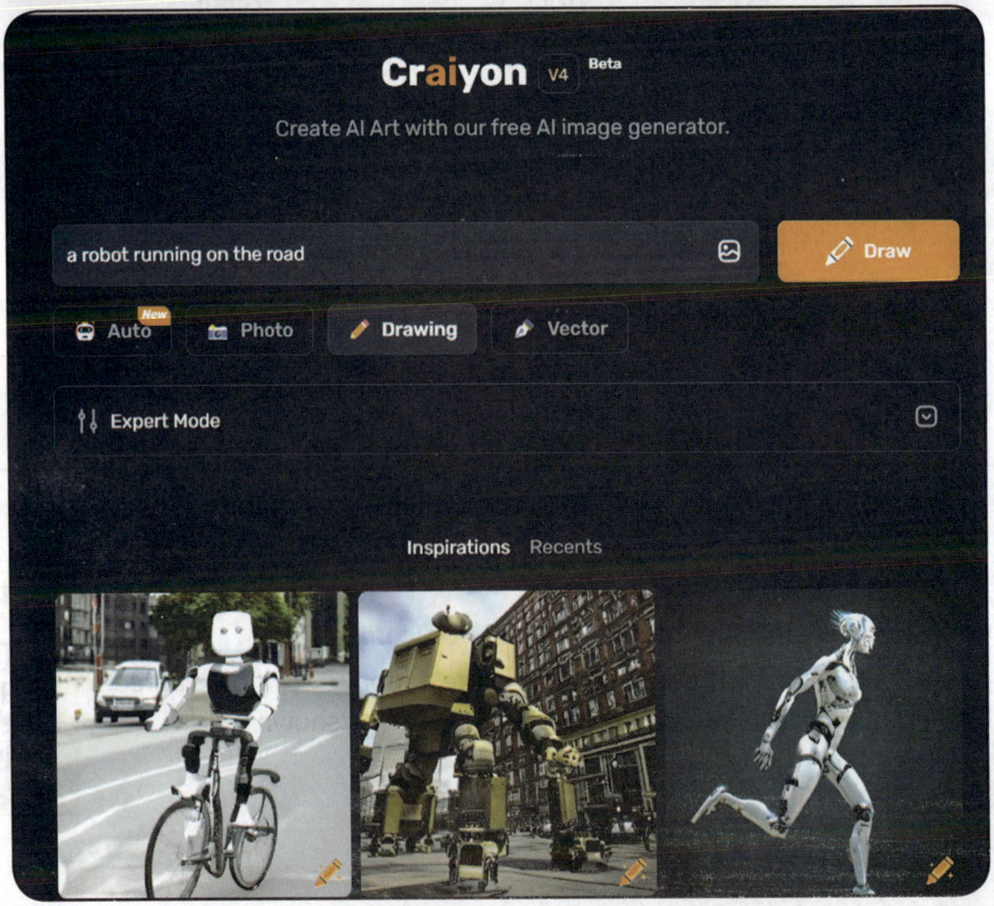
Craiyon V4 Beta
Create AI Art with our free AI image generator.
a robot running on the road
Draw
Auto New
Photo
Drawing
Vector
Expert Mode
Inspirations Recents

PREDICTIONS WITH AI

Predictions With AI
in Action

Scan QR Code

Watch the video and see how AI makes predictions.

Customised Ads

Summary Zone: Know about the meaning of AI

Activity 1: Scan and watch

Meaning of AI
in Action

Scan QR Code

AI General Intelligence

Neutralization Reaction
How to treat a bee sting?

Activity 2: What if Cats have Artificial Intelligence?

What if Cats have Artificial Intelligence in Action

Scan QR Code

Activity 3: Learn AIVA

AI-powered website that can compose classical and symphonic music. Based on deep learning algorithms, AIVA is the first AI tool to be credited as a composer for multiple projects. AIVA's music has been used in multiple soundtracks for films, advertisements, and video games.

AIVA in Action

Scan QR Code

1. Create your account by Log in.

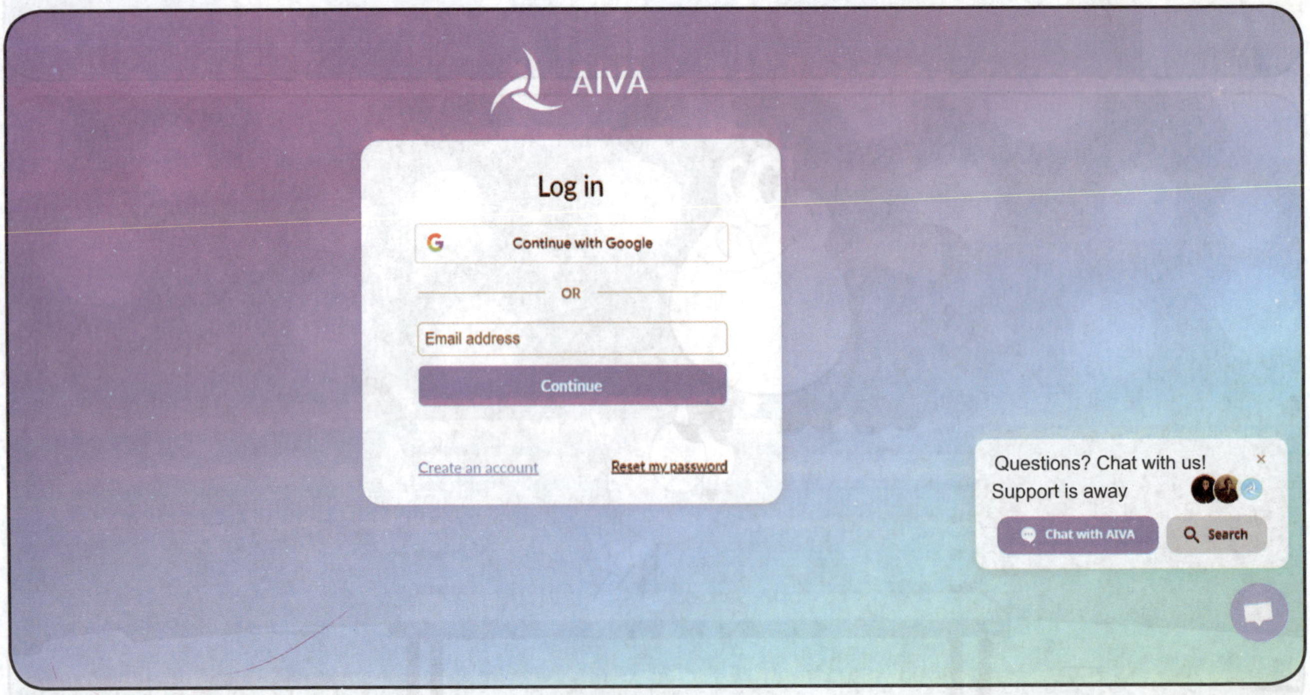

2. Agree and create your account.

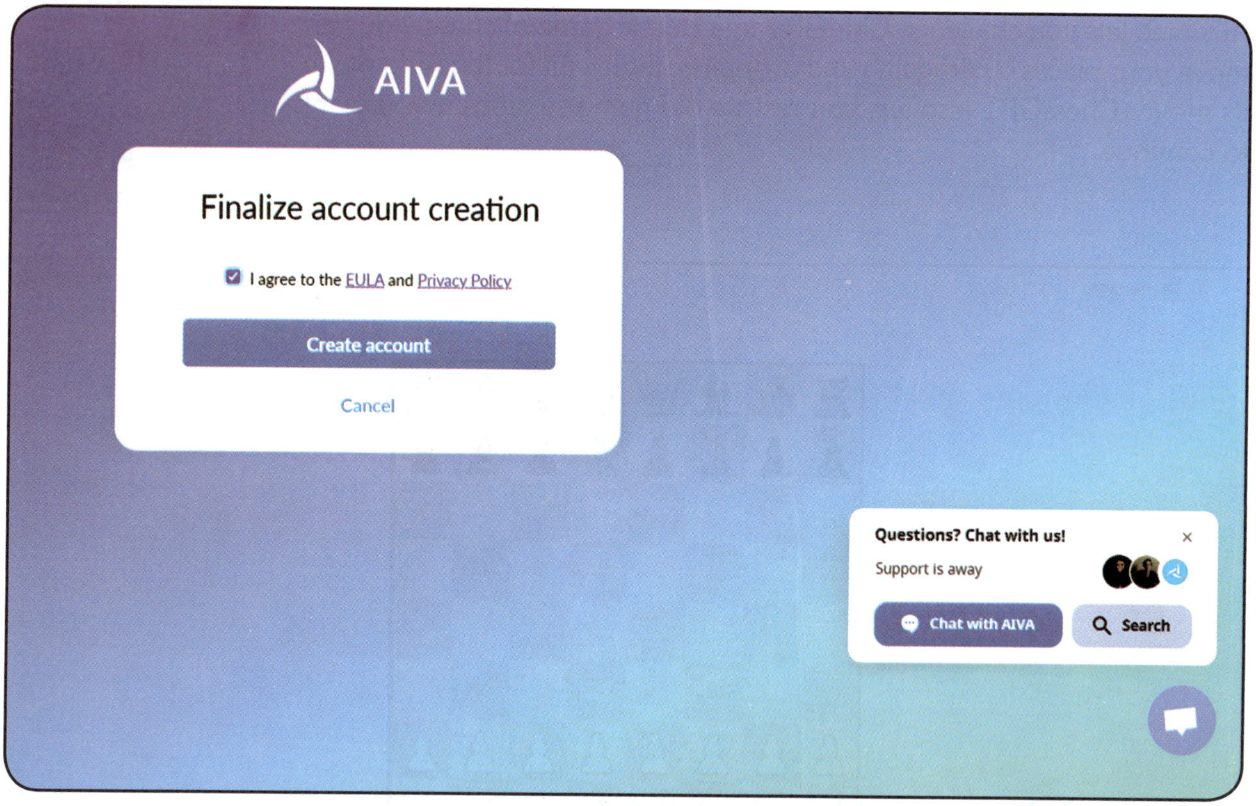

3. Create your track on composition tab and listen to a wonderful music.

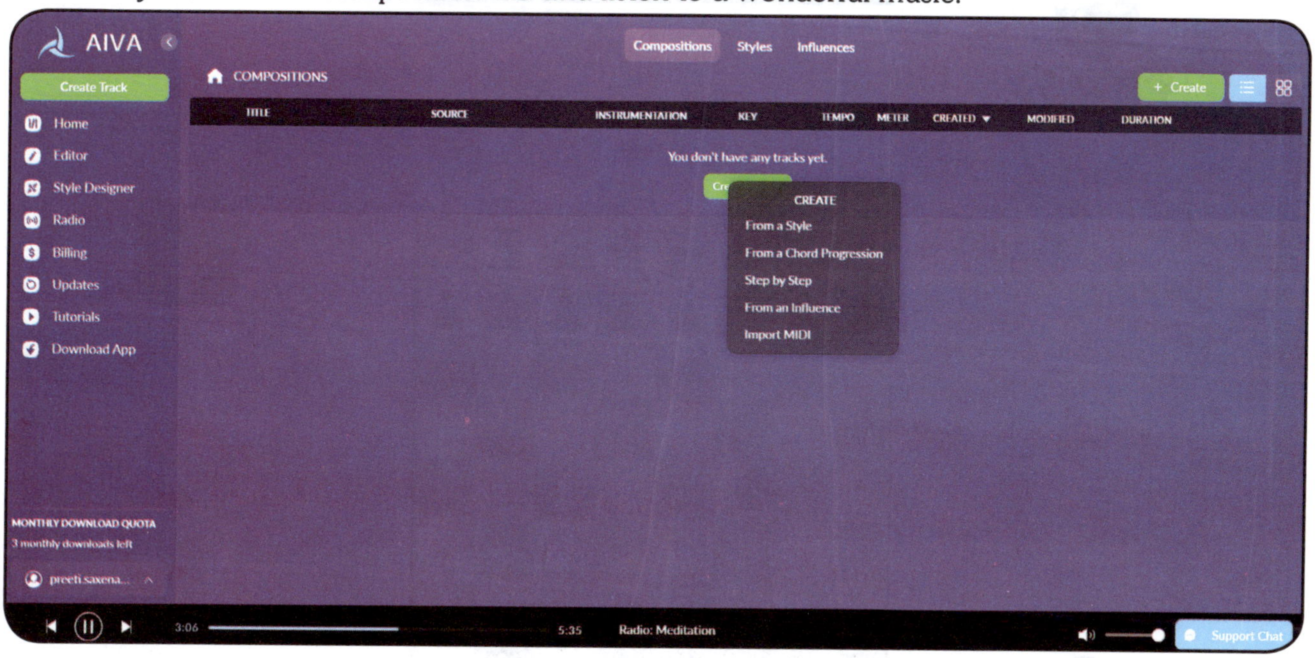

Activity 4: Learn Chess using ChessGPT. ChessGPT is a fun game of AI which lets you challenge ChatGPT to a classic game of chess. You can move your pieces by dragging and dropping, then wait for the AI to make its move. ChessGPT also lets you restore old game sessions if you want to continue.

ChessGPT in Action

Scan QR Code

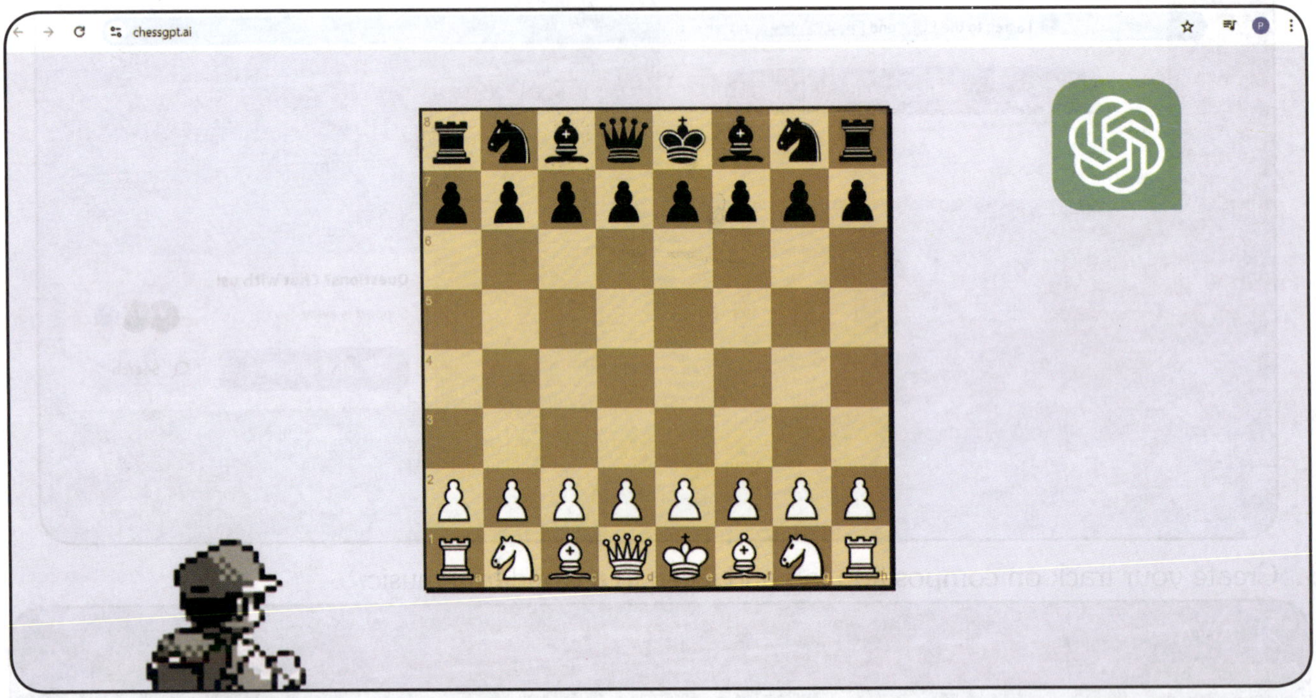

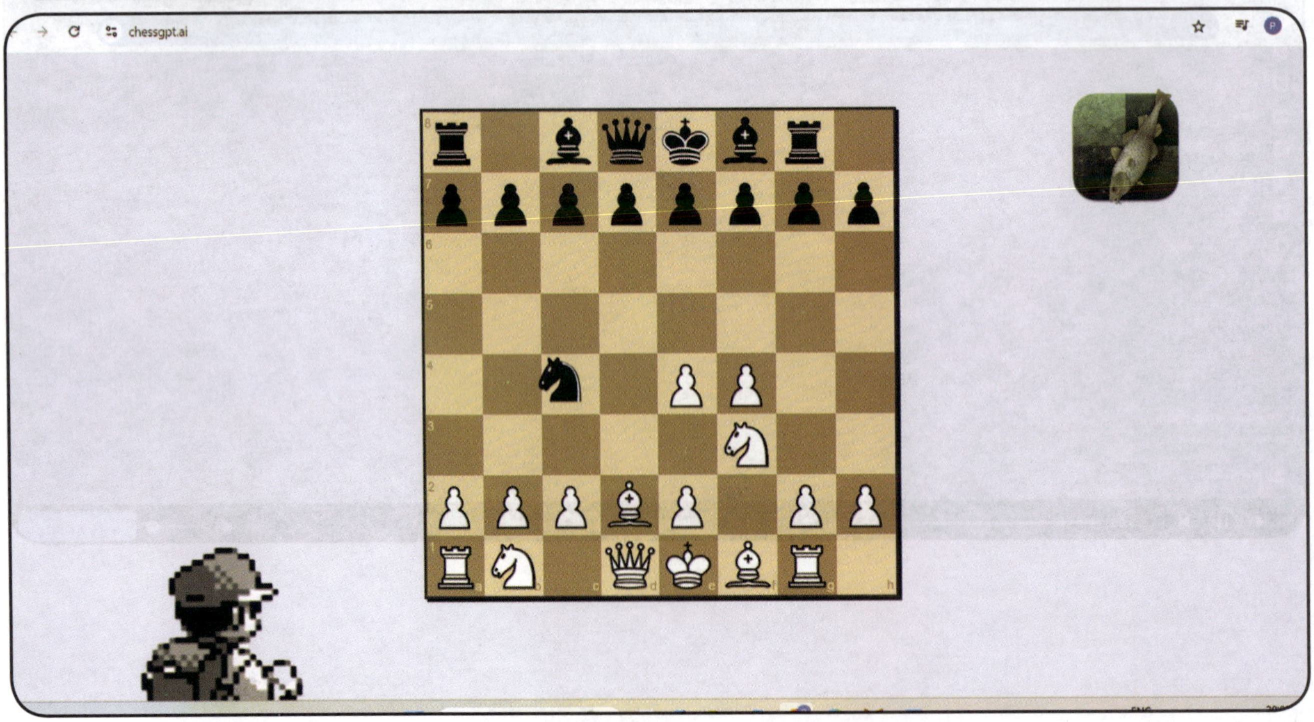

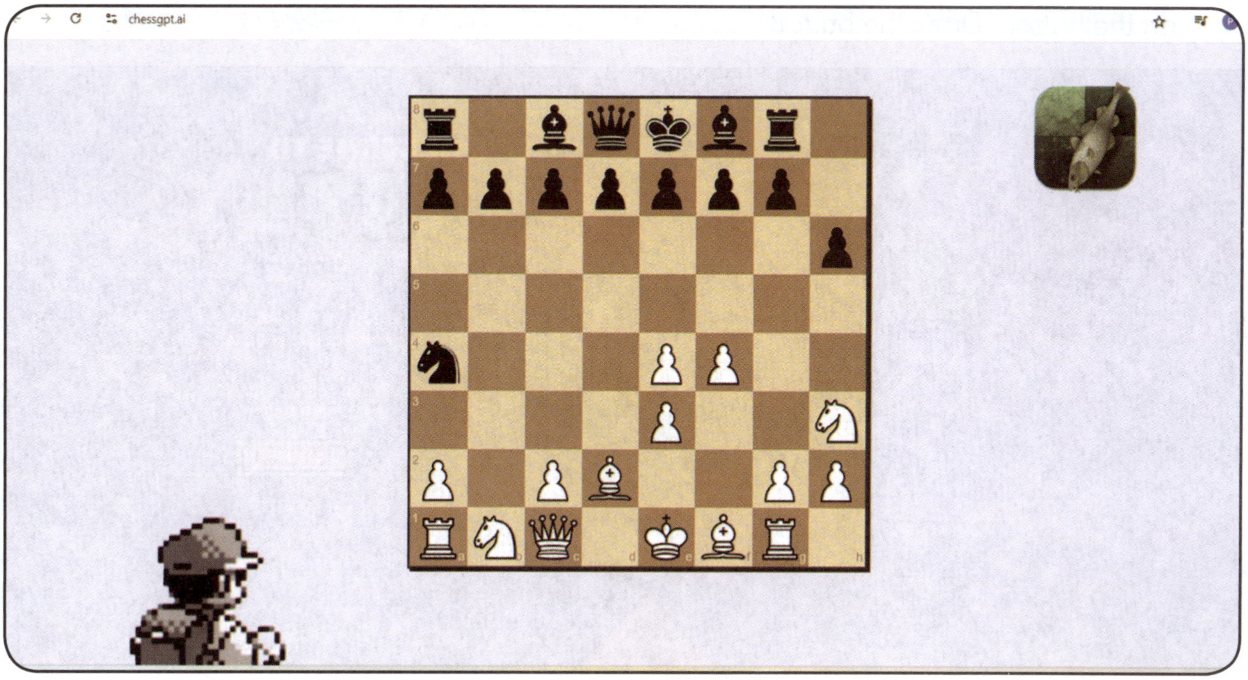

Activity 5: Choose and create by using PlayARTi.

ARTi is a fun AI image creator that lets you choose a character, location, and activity for your image. After choosing your options using the three buttons, you can click on "CREATE!" to get your unique image. PlayARTi is designed to be super easy to use, almost like a point-and-click adventure game!

PlayARTi
in Action

Scan QR Code

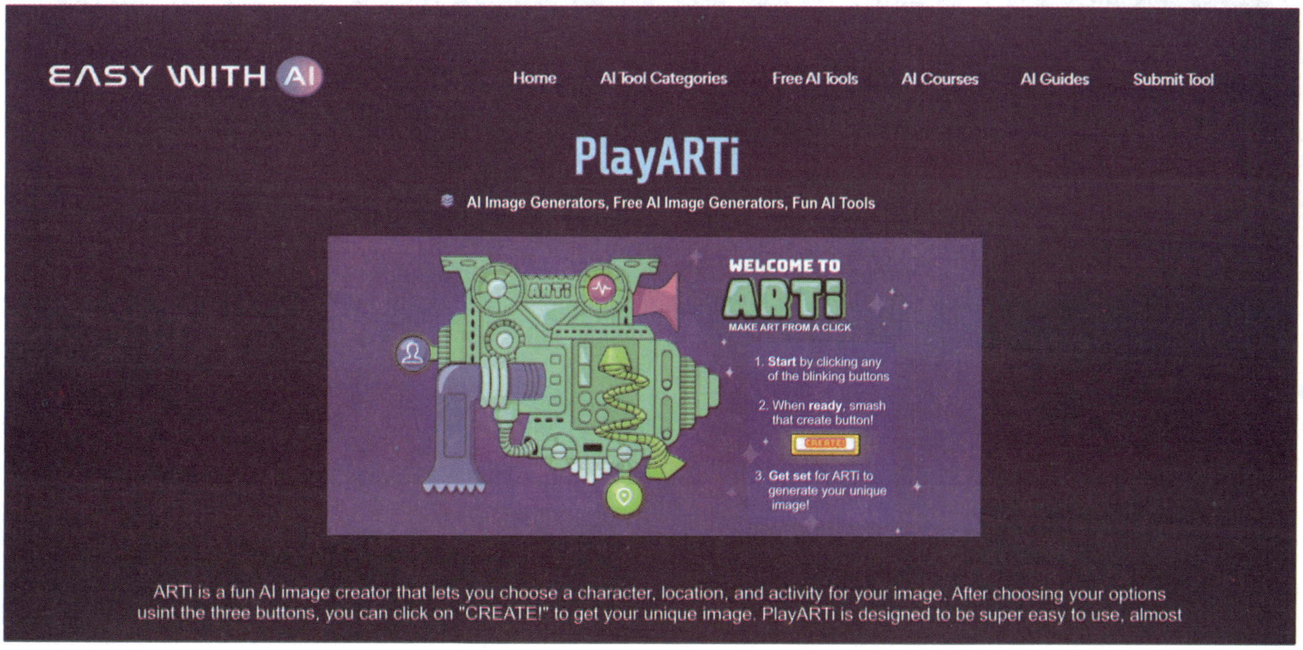

1. Click on the button. Draw the button

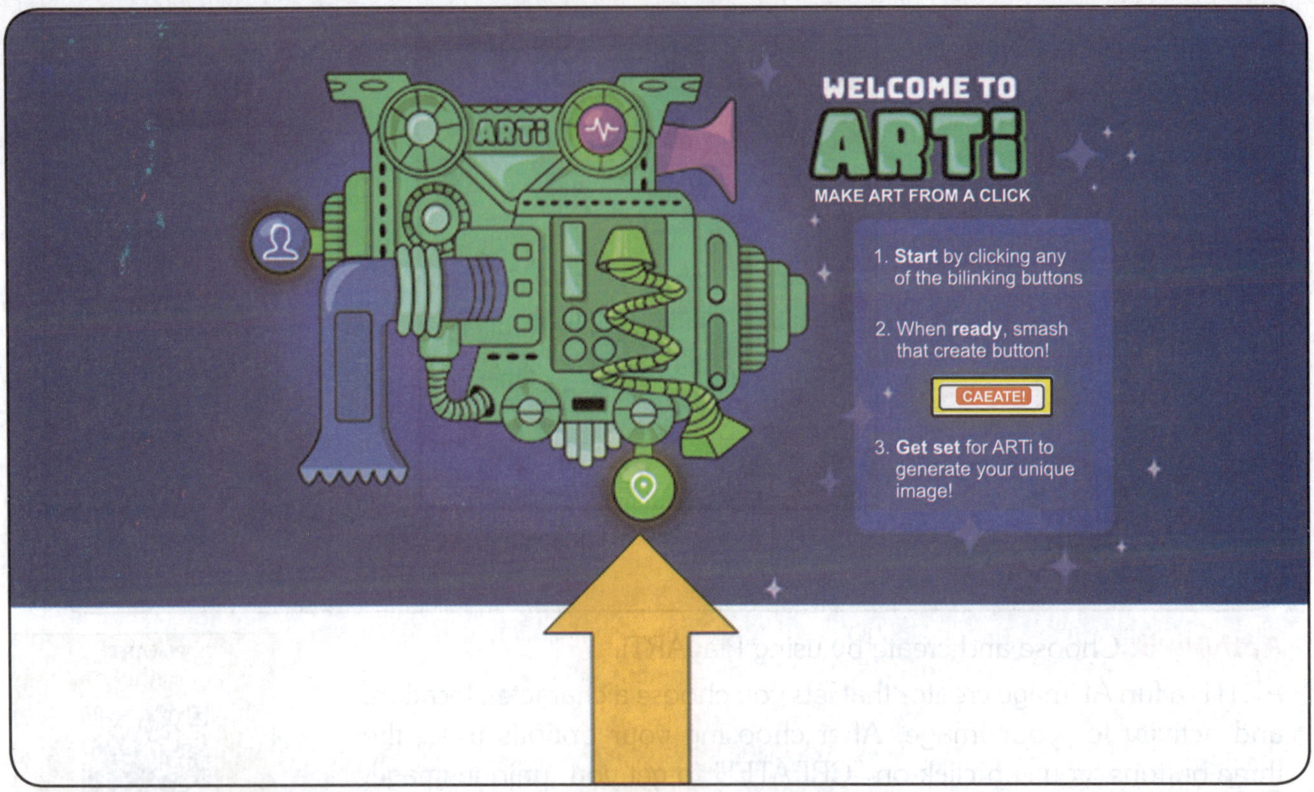

2. Choose the place.

3. Click on CREATE button.

The output is generated.

INTERESTING DIGITAL TERMS

1. **Digital Device:** Digital device is a piece of equipment like a computer, tablet, or smartphone that processes and stores information in the form of numbers (0s and 1s).

2. **Digital Footprint:** Digital footprints are the trail of data that people leave behind when they use the internet, such as the websites they visit or posts they make on social media.

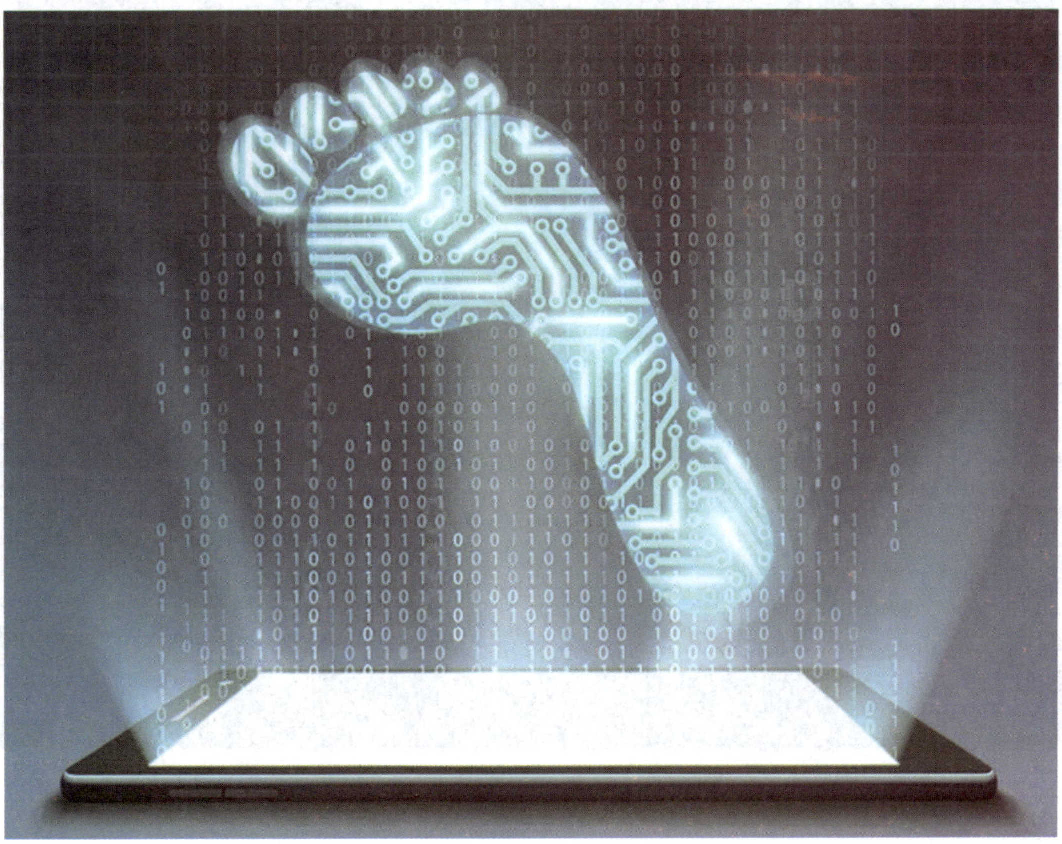

3. **Digital Literacy:** Digital literacy is the ability to use digital devices, the internet, and other technology safely and effectively to find, create, and share information.

4. **Digital Security:** Digital security involves taking measures to protect devices and data from getting damaged or accessed by unauthorized people, like using passwords or antivirus software.

5. **Digital Storage:** The place where data (like pictures, videos, and documents) is saved electronically, such as in a computer's hard drive or on cloud storage platforms.

6. **Digital Communication:** Sharing information using technology, like sending messages through email, social media, or chat apps.

7. **Digital Media:** Content that is shared or viewed using electronic devices, such as videos, music, and articles on websites.

8. **Digital Citizenship:** Acting responsibly and respectfully online, which includes being kind, not sharing harmful content, and protecting personal information.

9. **Digital Learning:** Using technology, like apps or websites, to study and complete schoolwork.

10. **Digital Currency:** A type of money that exists only in electronic form, like Bitcoin or digital payments made through apps like PayPal. The coins shown below do not exist in physical form.

LATEST AI TOOLS

Grammarly in Action

Scan QR Code

1. **Grammarly:** Grammarly is an AI-powered tool that checks spelling, grammar, and punctuation. It suggests corrections and explanations to help students to improve their writing. It can even suggest better word choices and offer style improvements, making it useful for school essays and homework.

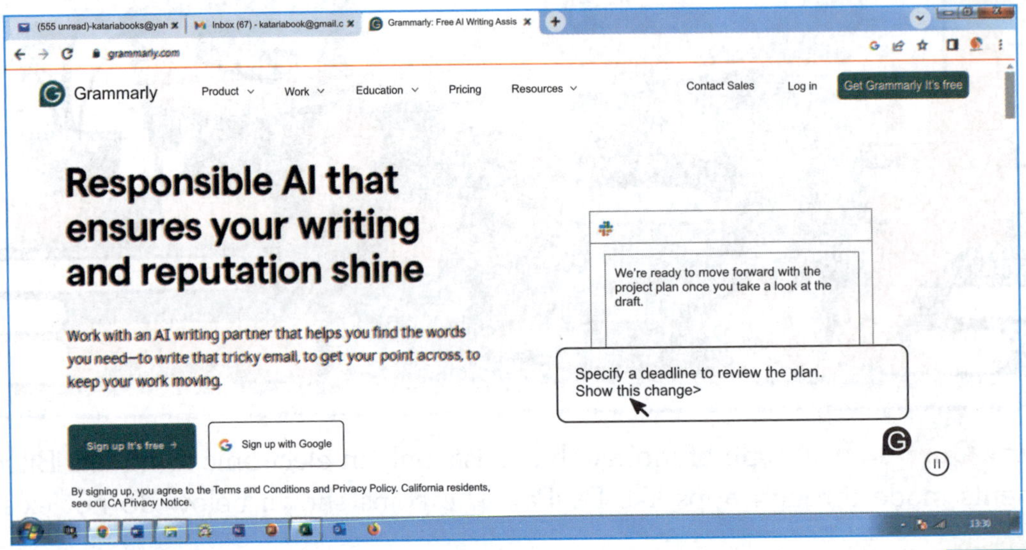

Khan Academy AI Tutor in Action

Scan QR Code

2. **Khan Academy AI Tutor:** Khan Academy now offers an AI-powered tutor named Khanmigo, which can help students with personalized learning. It uses AI to understand the student's progress, and based on that, offers hints, explanations, and even quizzes tailored to the student's needs. It is useful for maths, science, and other subjects.

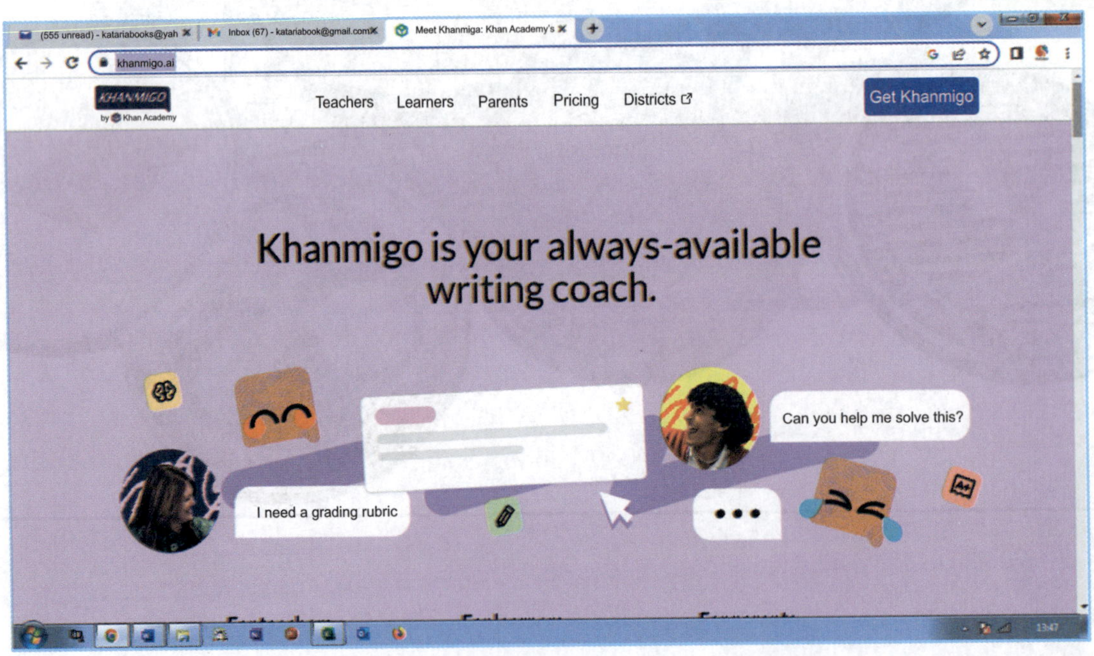

3. Google Lens: Google Lens allows students to use their phone camera to scan maths problems, questions, or images, and get immediate explanations and information. It uses AI to recognize objects, text, and mathematical problems, making it easier to find answers or explanations quickly.

Google Lens in Action

Scan QR Code

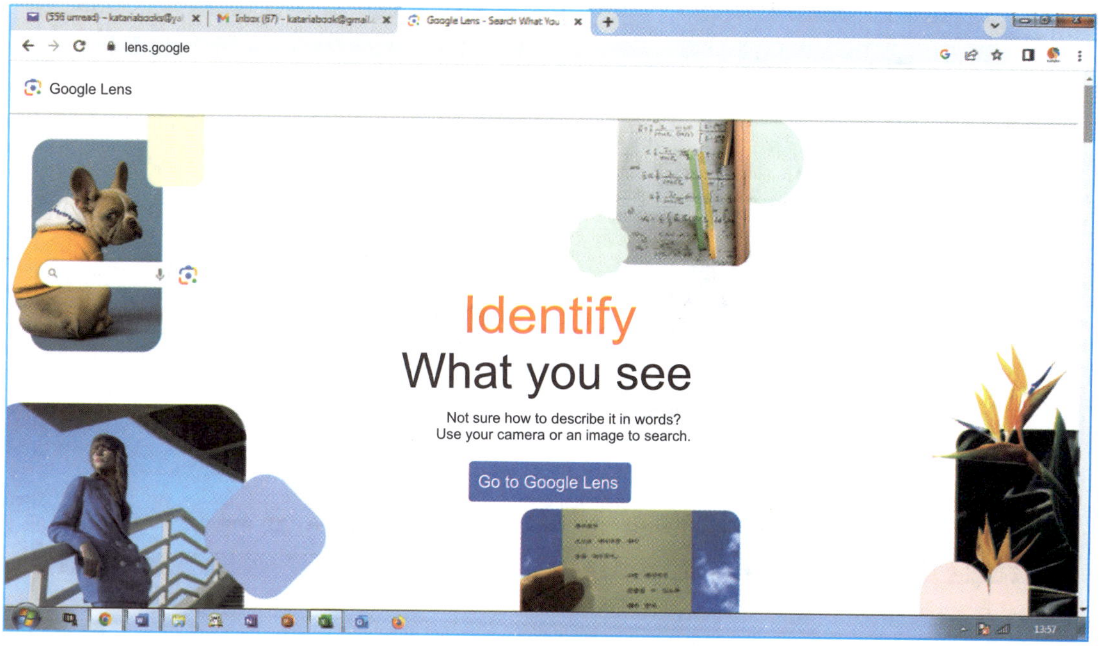

4. Socratic by Google: Socratic is a free AI-powered learning app. Students can take pictures of homework questions, and Socratic provides step-by-step explanations and resources to help them understand the topic. It is particularly helpful for maths, science, and history homework.

Socratic by Google in Action

Scan QR Code

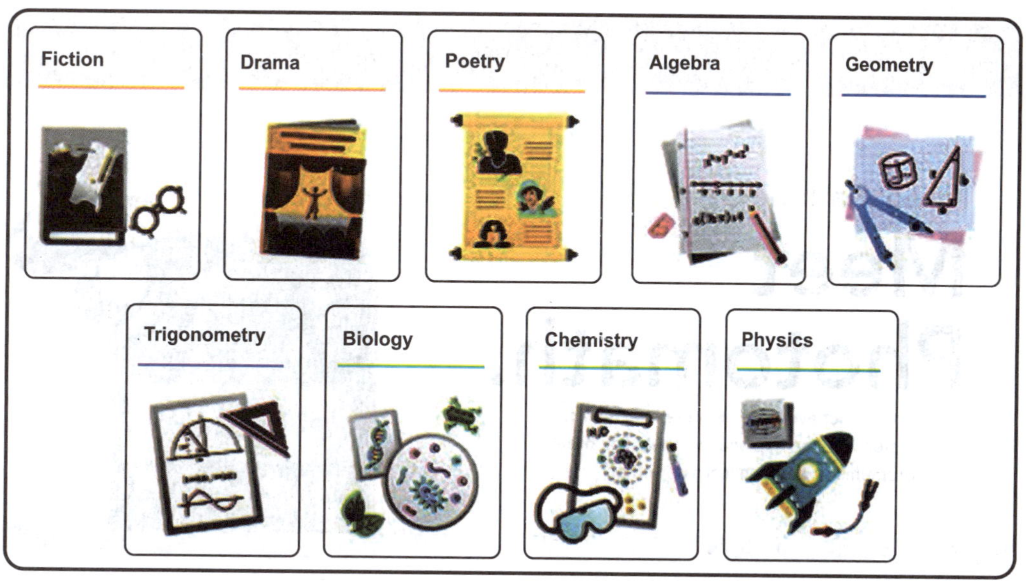

Duolingo
in Action
Scan QR Code

5. **Duolingo:** Duolingo uses AI to help students learn new languages through gamified lessons. The AI tracks the student's progress and adjusts the difficulty of questions based on their learning pace. It also uses spaced repetition to help with language retention.

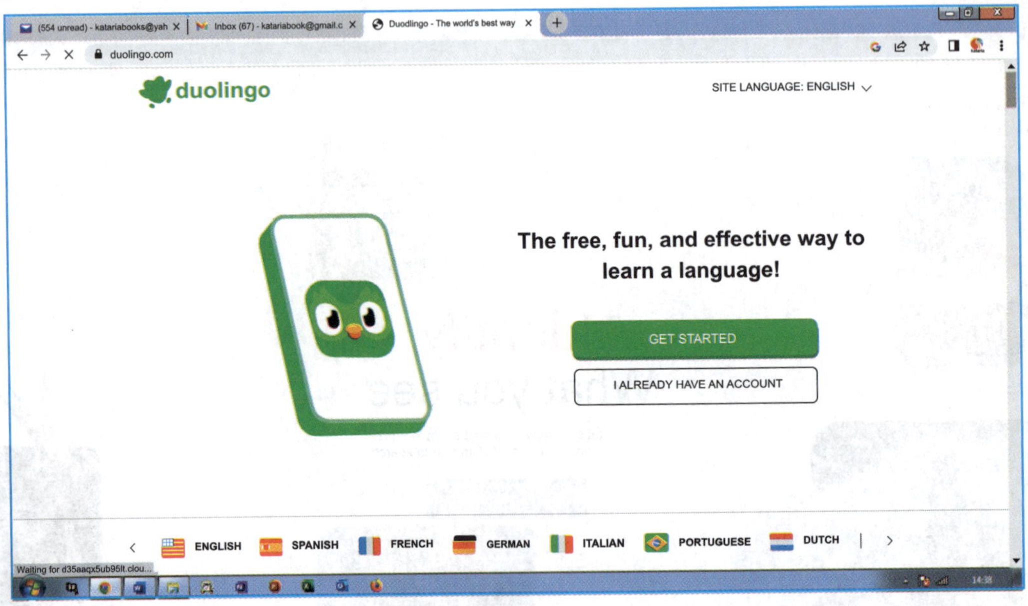

Photomath
in Action
Scan QR Code

6. **Photomath:** Photomath is an AI-powered mathematical problem solver. Students can scan handwritten or printed maths problems with their phone camera, and the app will show step-by-step solutions. It is helpful for understanding how to solve different types of maths problems.

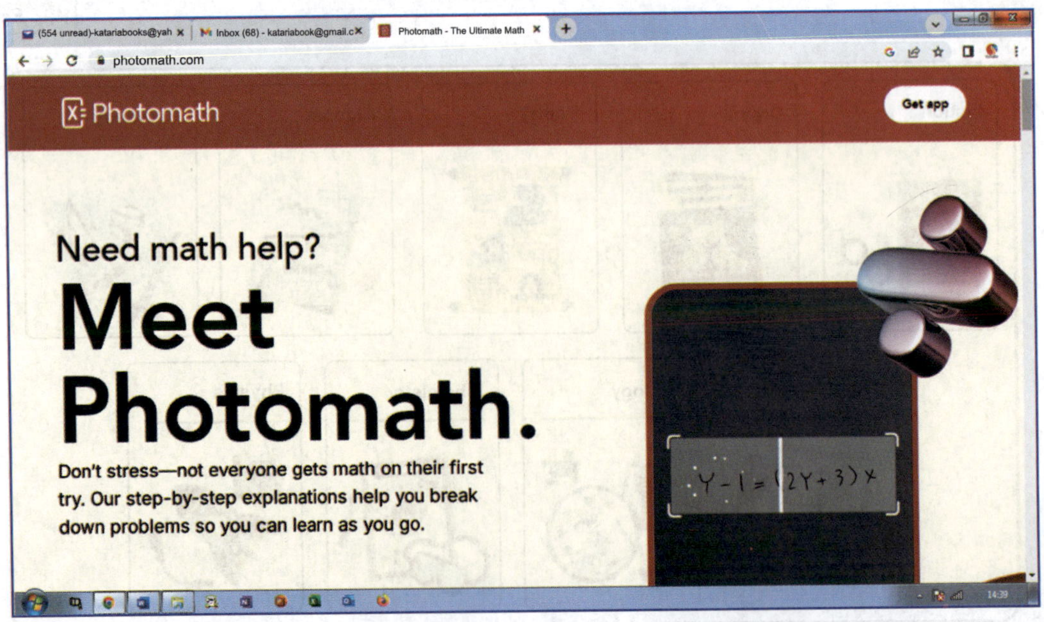

7. **Quizlet:** Quizlet uses AI to create custom flashcards and quizzes for students. It also has a feature called "Learn Mode" that adjusts the difficulty of questions based on how well the student is doing. The AI tracks performance and helps students in reviewing concepts they struggle with.

Quizlet in Action

Scan QR Code

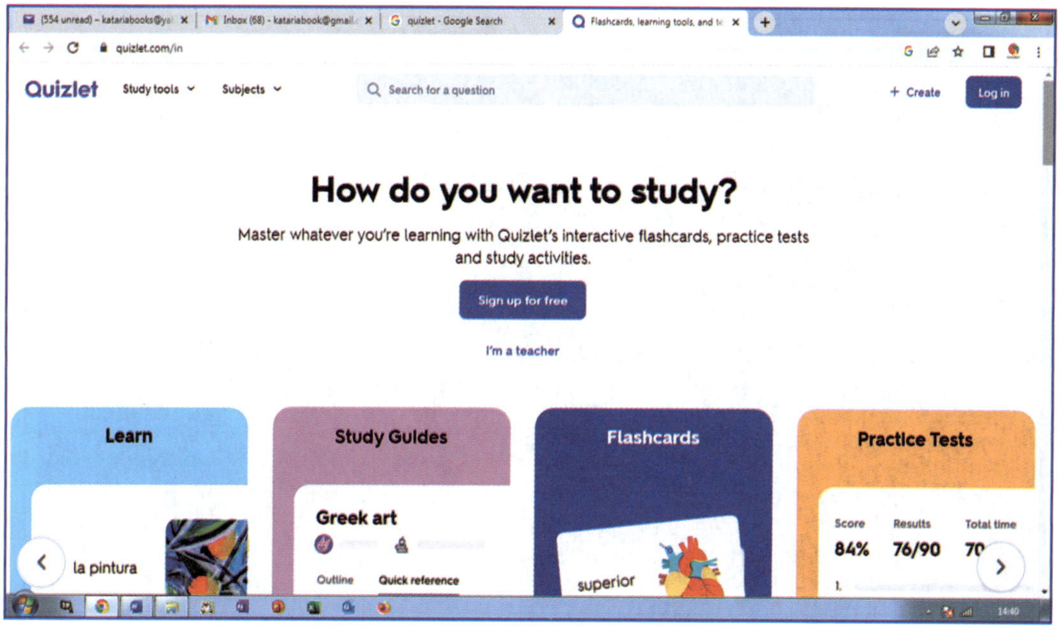

8. **Brainly:** Brainly is an AI-powered homework help platform where students can ask questions and receive answers from experts or peers. AI filters out incorrect answers and suggests helpful solutions based on the difficulty level of the questions.

Brainly in Action

Scan QR Code

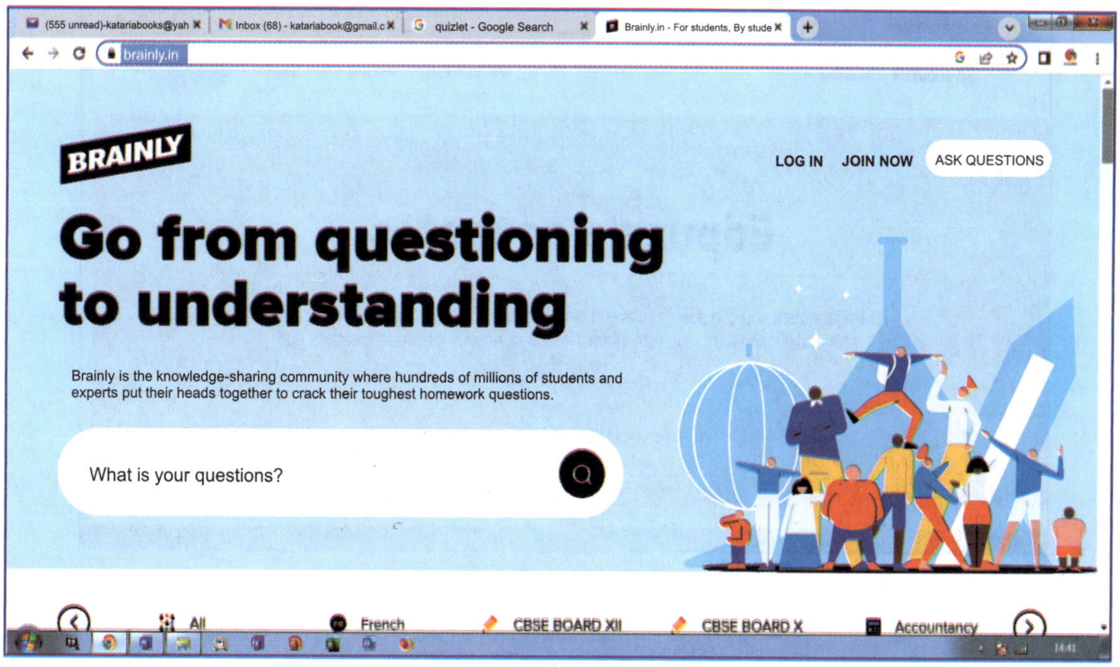

Tynker
in Action
Scan QR Code

9. **Tynker:** Tynker is an AI-enhanced platform that teaches coding and computer science through games and puzzles. The AI tracks a student's progress and adjusts the challenges to keep the learning fun and engaging.

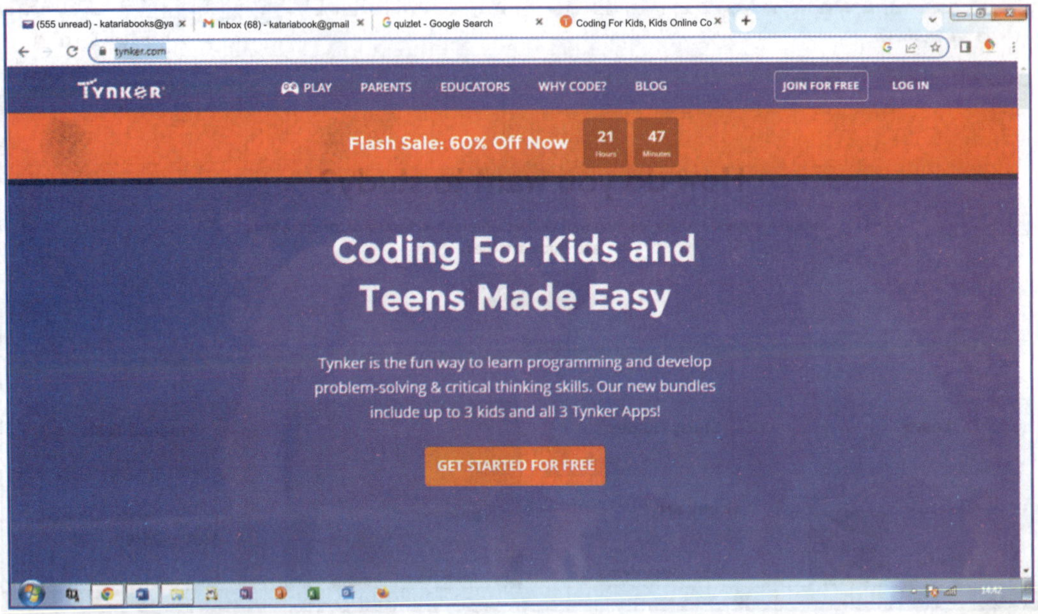

Edpuzzle
in Action
Scan QR Code

10. **Edpuzzle:** Edpuzzle uses AI to turn videos into interactive learning experiences. Teachers can embed questions into videos, and students can answer them while watching. AI tracks the student's progress and provides immediate feedback to both students and teachers.

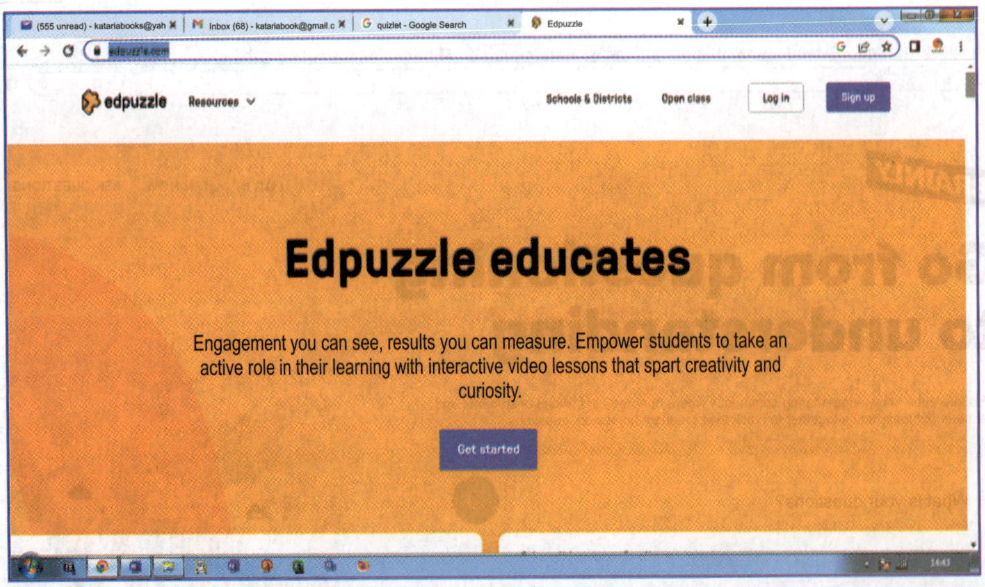

Win Prizes

ATTENTION READERS

Win Prizes

We request for your frank assessment regarding various aspects of the book as given below:

A TEXTBOOK OF ARTIFICIAL INTELLIGENCE

(Unlocking the Secrets of AI)

Subject Code: 901A | Skill Education

(As per Latest NEP Guidelines)

Class VI

By: Preeti Saxena

Please Fill up the Sheet in Neat and Clean Writing

(i) What topics of your syllabus, important for your examination point of view, are not covered in this book?

....

(ii) What are the chapters wherein the treatment of the subject matter is not systematic or organised or updated?

....

(iii) Have you come across misprints/mistakes/factual inaccuracies in the book? Please specify the chapters and the page numbers.

....

(iv) What other books on the same subject have you found/heard better than the present book? Please specify in terms of price and quality.

....

(v) Further suggestions and comments for the improvement of this book.

....

(vi) Who recommended you this book? (Please tick (✓) in the box near the option relevant to you.

Teacher ☐ Friends ☐ Bookseller ☐

(vii) Name of the recommending teacher, his designation and address:

....

(viii) Name and address of the bookseller you purchased the book from :

....

(ix) Name and address of your institution (Please mention the University or Board as the case may be)

....

(x) Your name and complete postal address:

....

(xi) Course you are enrolled in:

....

The best assessment will be awarded each month: The award will be in the form of our publications as decided by the Editorial Board.

Please mail the filled up coupon at your earliest to:

(PS: If need be please attach a separate sheet to write your views)

S.K. KATARIA & SONS®
4885/109, Prakash Mahal, Dr. Subhash Bhargav Lane,
Opposite Delhi Medical Association, Daryaganj, New Delhi–110002 (INDIA)
Phone: +91-11-43551243, Mobile: +91-9871775858, 7678425209
e-mail: katariabook@gmail.com, katariabooks@yahoo.com
Website: www.skkatariaandsons.com